WHAT INDIA
AND VIRGIN MARY
HAVE IN COMMON

ALSO BY M. P. PRABHAKARAN

Racist Bones in
President Trump's Body

What I Learned from
My Thirty-Day European Odyssey

Letters on India
The New York Times *Did Not Publish*

The Historical Origin of India's Underdevelopment:
A World-System Perspective

WHAT INDIA
AND VIRGIN MARY
HAVE IN COMMON

M.P. PRABHAKARAN

ARPress
45 Dan Road Suite 5
Canton MA 02021
Hotline: 1(888) 821-0229
Fax: 1(508) 545-7580

Ordering Information:
Quantity sales. Special discounts are available on quantity purchases by corporations, associations, and others. For details, contact the publisher at the address above.

Printed in the United States of America.

ISBN-13:   Softcover   979-8-89356-297-2
              eBook   979-8-89356-296-5

Library of Congress Control Number: 2024903320

For the memory of my late brother
M. P. RAMACHANDRAN

Table of Contents

PICTURES

Preface

"I travel, therefore I am – apologies to Descartes for twisting his noble thought." This has been my stock reply to those who ask me where I get the guts from to venture into far corners of the world, often alone.

The venture is a belated realization of a dream I have nurtured since my early teens. While most other dreams I nurtured have shattered, this one remained intact. I am happy that, at long last, I am in the process of realizing it. The joy I am deriving from the process more than makes up for the agony I felt when my other dreams got shattered. I am happy that things turned out the way they did.

Apart from being a source of great pleasure, traveling has also been my greatest learning experience in life. If academic qualifications are a measure of one's learning, I have a string of them, including a Ph.D. in Political Science from The New School for Social Research, New York. But what I learned at The New School, a prestigious American institution, and, before that, at various institutions in India, is no match for what I did from my travels around the world.

The most valuable lesson I learned is that people are people, no matter what region or religion they belong to or what political system they live under. They open up to you if you approach them with an open mind.

I did not begin pursuing my passion for travel with a view to writing a book about it. The excitement I felt, the knowledge I gained, and the friendships I built with people from vastly different cultures around the world have been rewards enough for me. The book materialized as an afterthought.

Some of my friends, to whom I used to send emails narrating my experience and sharing my excitement, responded with gratitude, and kept asking for more of them. "M.P., travel writing is your forte," one of them said. "Some of the pieces you have sent are so heart-warming. Why not concentrate on this field? Why waste time belaboring with political stuff?"

She has been familiar with my political writings, the targets of which often are pompous asses who pretend to have solutions for all problems in the world. Since 2001, those writings have been appearing in *The East-West Inquirer*, an online monthly I started that year.

Thanks to friends like her, I started publishing in the monthly some of my travel writings, too. The responses from those who regularly visit my website, www.eastwestinquirer.com, have been exhilarating. Some of them suggested that I publish those articles in the form of a book. I owe this book to those friends' suggestion.

It was first published in 2012, under the title *Capitalism Comes to Mao's Mausoleum*. What I am bringing you now is an expanded, and slightly edited, version of it.

1

My Two Embarrassing
Moments in Buenos Aires

San Telmo is to Buenos Aires what Greenwich Village is to New York City. Both are known for their Sunday flea markets, antiques shops, art galleries, street performances and such other attractions. Tourists to the two cities make it a point to visit the two neighborhoods before they leave for other destinations.

For visitors to Buenos Aires, the Argentine capital, who are looking for the city's old-world charm, there are 19th-century colonial mansions, famed for their grandiose architecture, on both sides of the streets in San Telmo. Most of the streets are paved with cobblestones. The mansions were, once upon a time, owned and occupied by upper-class Spaniards. To meet the housing needs of the new waves of immigrants, mostly Italians, many of those mansions were later converted into multifamily apartment complexes. Lately, some of the mansions have also been converted into shops, art galleries, restaurants, and bars.

Frolicking Argentines and fun-loving tourists bring San Telmo to life, especially on Sunday evenings. Adding to the fun and frolic is that world-famous dance the Argentine culture is inseparable from. The dance – yes, you have guessed it right – is the tango.

Tango dancers from various parts of Buenos Aires and beyond flock to San Telmo and perform at street corners and sidewalks. They do it partly in keeping up with an age-old tradition, but mostly to make a living by entertaining tourists. Some of these street performers are just as good as the famous tango dancers who perform at various night clubs in Buenos Aires. Watching the tango at night clubs would cost one anywhere between 20 and 100 U.S. dollars, depending on the popularity of the club and professional standing of the dancers. At San Telmo street corners, the cost is what one decides and can afford – an important factor that went into my opting for that place, rather than a night club.

I love the tango, especially the Argentine tango. I wanted to learn it ever since I was first exposed to it. Somehow, I never got down to doing it. Little did I know when I set out for San Telmo on that Sunday evening that my favorite dance was also going to give me one of the most embarrassing moments in my life.

Most of the dancers that I saw at various street corners were in compatible pairs. By which I mean that there were no same-sex couples. One could tell from their performances that they had put into them a lot of planning and practicing. There were also dancers who would start the show solo and then persuade one of the spectators to join him or her as partner. "Another cost-cutting device in a country that is financially strapped?" I wondered. I dismissed the thought as fast as it came, reasoning: "Audience participation has always been an essential feature of street performances in every country and every culture."

My First Lesson in Tango

Some of the spectators who volunteered to participate were excellent dancers themselves. But those who did it only after a good deal of persuading by the street performers were pathetic to watch.

I was thoroughly enjoying the evening, taking in the sights and sounds of the cultural corner of Buenos Aires, when a cross-dressed woman performer caught my attention. In a double-breasted coat with a matching tie and a hat, and with a moustache waxed to keep its handlebar shape intact, she could probably be imitating an English country gentleman. (Many Argentines do imitate Europeans, making them the butt of jokes among other South Americans.) I stopped to watch her.

As the cliché goes, it took two to tango. I was curious to find out whom, from among the spectators, the performer would pick for her partner – the actual opposite sex or the opposite sex which the man she was masquerading as called for? The curiosity turned into shock and fright when her choice fell on me.

My protestations, in English, that I hardly knew any steps were dismissed by her, in Spanish. I thought she said, "It doesn't matter." She dragged me to the center of the dance area, to the delight of the crowd. The crowd clapped and whistled.

"Shouldn't the partner be of the opposite sex in appearance, too?" I shouted, to no one in particular.

"Come on, man, be a good sport," one from the crowd shouted back.

He had a British accent. The crowd that gathered there consisted of various nationalities.

The first thing the performer did was to press me against her taut breasts. That part, I must say, I thoroughly enjoyed. The handlebar moustache that brushed against my cheek did not diminish the enjoyment one bit.

But her next gesture made it clear that I was not to get too excited about that physical contact. She pointed two fingers toward her eyes, meaning that I was supposed to look straight into her eyes. Which I did – nervously. Then she began to push me around, telling me – in Spanish, of course – which leg to move first, and in what direction. I nodded yes, though I didn't understand a word of what she said. I was anxious to get it over with fast. The instructions ended with her asking me to fall on her right arm and throw my right leg up, with toes pointing to the sky, which was the usual finale of a tango dance. Only then did I realize that she was expecting me to play the female role.

She turned the boom box on, and the music began to blare. Once again, she held me tight. And once again, I could feel her breasts rubbing against my chest. But this time, I was too nervous to derive any pleasure out of it. She nudged me to take the first step.

My first step, in the first tango dance in my life, on my first visit to the land of the tango! Never had I imagined that it was also going to be my last step for quite some time. My left heel fell on the toes of her right leg and nearly crushed them.

She roared in pain. And I profusely apologized. My explanation that the step mix-up was caused by the sex mix-up did not have any effect on her. She pushed me toward the spectators.

The spectators roared, too, but in exultation – and to my great embarrassment. If they had come out that evening to have a good time, I didn't disappoint them.

As soon as the performer picked another partner from the crowd and I knew that nobody was watching me, I quietly withdrew from the scene.

I rushed to a nearby sidewalk café and ordered a cool Argentine beer. The beer was very satisfying.

Visit to a Turkish Bath

I had one more embarrassing experience during my 2001 Buenos Aires trip. It happened at a Turkish bath. When the hotel I was staying in offered a free Turkish bath as part of the deal, I said to myself, "At long last, I am going to have the ecstatic experience I have been dreaming about all my life!" Until then, I had only seen it in movies and read about it.

The bath facility took up nearly a quarter of the hotel's basement. The huge hall that led to the actual bath had a bar on one side and a locker room on the other. As I entered the hall, my stare fell on a group of men sitting around a table, drinking beer and playing cards. All of them were tall, old and fat. Those physical features were not what caused my stare, though. It was their nonchalant attitude to what they were exposing to one another. The towels they might have been wearing were lying beside them. They were wet, which made me guess that the men had just come out of the bath.

When the bartender saw my surprised look, he pointed his thumb toward the locker room. I knew what he meant. He meant not merely that I must be heading in the direction of the locker room. He also meant that I was being stupid staring at his patrons the way I was doing.

Inside the locker room, there were men, most of them old, walking in and out of small cubicles. Only a few of them had towels wrapped around their waists. Others carried them in their hands. They couldn't care less that an Indian was amused by what was dangling in front of them. This time, I tried hard not to show any surprise. I didn't want the locker room attendant to repeat to me what the bartender had done only a couple of minutes earlier. The attendant handed a huge towel for me to change into and showed me the room where I would be having the actual steam bath.

As I entered the hot, steamy room, I saw several men sitting on benches. Some of them were completely naked and others partially so. They were also unconcerned about what they were displaying. One look at them, and I said to myself: "I am no match for any of these guys. Let me not reveal to them that I come from an underdeveloped country."

I made for the exit fast, making sure that my towel was firmly in place.

2

Eva Peron's Tomb Is Too Small for Her Ego

It was November 2001. I had been in Buenos Aires for five days, enjoying everything I saw around. I was surprised to see that, in spite of the economic woes the country had been experiencing, the capital city functioned fairly efficiently and its reputation as "The Paris of South America" remained intact.

Even before I arrived in Buenos Aires, the international media had been full of stories foreboding Argentina's economic doom. At the time I was there, the International Monetary Fund had been meeting in Ottawa, Canada, to explore ways of saving Argentina the embarrassment of defaulting on its debt repayment to lending institutions.

As it turned out later, the IMF's efforts were of no avail: Argentina did default, in December 2001, on its public debt of US$141 billion, thereby besmirching its name in the comity of nations. Sovereign default is something no nation would find easy to live with.

In Buenos Aires and other major cities of the country, people took to the streets almost daily – demanding jobs, back wages, the money they had deposited in banks and, sometimes, even food. Riots resulting from the crisis claimed scores of lives.

When I was in Buenos Aires, however, the only visible signs of the economic gloom I noticed were empty tables in restaurants and an occasional beggar on the street. Sometimes the beggars, almost all of them kids, approached customers in restaurants, too. I mean those restaurants that were lucky enough to have some customers.

I saw a few beggars holding fliers with stories of their privation printed on them. Some customers would give them a coin or two without even looking at the fliers. Some others would shoo the intruders away.

One customer who gave a kid a small-size coin learned to his disappointment later that it was of five-peso denomination. The Argentine peso, at the time, was linked to the American dollar and equal in par value. The customer had stupidly thought that the smallness in size of the coin meant smallness in value.

Street Performers on Avenida 9 de Julio

There were also those who, strictly speaking, couldn't be called beggars. Though their nuisance value was the same as that of beggars, they did provide some entertainment in return for what they were asking. They should be called street performers.

Most of them chose the widest avenue in Buenos Aires for their performance. The wider the avenue, the longer would be the traffic halt at pedestrian crossings. The widest avenue in Buenos Aires is Avenida 9 de Julio (July 9 Avenue). With 12 lanes, six each going in either direction, it is the widest avenue I have seen in any city anywhere in the world. The avenue is named after the country's Independence Day. Argentina gained independent from Spanish colonial rule on July 9, 1816.

The performers would wait at corners where July 9 Avenue intersects with other streets and other avenues. As soon as the traffic light turned red, they would jump from the sidewalk onto the avenue, in front of the first row of vehicles, and begin their performance – juggling balls or sticks, torch display, dancing or just clowning around. They would have as much time for their performance as it took for pedestrians to cross the 12-lane avenue and its green-patch separation in the middle. A few seconds before the traffic light changed back to green, they would stop their performance and approach the occupants of vehicles with a hat in hand. I wondered whether those teenage artistes and acrobats were able to make a living doing what they were doing. Most motorists ignored them, and some even stared and shouted at them.

After savoring the sights and sounds of Buenos Aires for five days, I felt that I hadn't had enough. I wanted to see more of the city and surrounding areas. I wanted to visit San Telmo and watch the tango a few more times. So the day before I was scheduled to fly out, I went to the Varig Airlines office to enquire whether postponing my departure by a few days would cost me anything extra.

I was sitting at the airlines' office, waiting for my turn to be called at the reservation desk. The wait had become too long, and I was getting bored. I turned to a woman sitting next to me and asked whether she spoke English.

"What a relief!" I said when she replied yes. "Those who speak English are very few around here."

I could tell from the way she looked at me that she didn't like my remark. While my question was a legitimate one, especially in a country whose native language is Spanish, the remark I made in response to her reply smacked of superciliousness. How stupid of me to make such a remark! When I made it, I had in my hand a copy of *Buenos Aires Herald*, an English daily published from the Argentine capital. I should have known that it was published primarily for locals like her, and not tourists like me. I was relieved when she laughed away my faux pas and decided to continue the conversation.

"You Are No Gandhi"

"Are you from India?" she asked me.

I have been asked "Are you from India?" in various parts of the world. And every time I heard that question, my stock reply has been: "Yes, originally from India, but now I live in the United States." But this time the question has a special effect on me because it came from a person living in a place where Indians are a rarity. She not only impressed me with her question, but also endeared herself to me with what she said after I gave her my stock reply.

"You are no Gandhi. I can tell," she said, her eyes narrowing into a squint, waiting for my reaction.

I played along, saying, "You are absolutely right. If I were Gandhi, I would be living in India and doing something for the millions of the less fortunate who are living there."

Gandhi was very much on her mind, she said, because she had just finished reading the Spanish version of *Freedom at Midnight*. She also said that she had been a great admirer of Gandhi since her childhood. "My admiration went up after reading the book," she added.

Freedom at Midnight, by Larry Collins and Dominique Lapierre, published in the mid-1970s, is a fascinating portrayal of India's freedom struggle. Gandhi dominates the book from beginning to end. The Argentine admirer of Gandhi also told me what she thought about the other personalities that figure prominently in the book: Jawaharlal Nehru, Muhammad Ali Jinnah and Louis Mountbatten.

She thanked me for correcting her, when she said that Mountbatten was the only one among them who was still alive. "He died in 1979 in a bomb explosion," I told her. "He was sailing on his pleasure boat, off the coast of Ireland, when it happened. It was found out later that the bomb had been planted on the boat by terrorists belonging to the Irish Republican Army."

La Recoleta Cemetery

We talked about many more things. The blunder with which I started the conversation notwithstanding, a rapport began to develop between us. She gave me the addresses of a few must-see places in Buenos Aires and then asked: "Have you visited the cemetery of the rich and famous in Argentina?"

She was referring to La Recoleta Cemetery, a visit to which is invariably included in all conducted tours of Buenos Aires. The cemetery is 13½ acres in area and considered the costliest piece of real estate in all of Argentina. It has rows and rows of mausoleums, built in memory of many famous (and infamous) people in Argentina's history – presidents, politicians, soldiers, authors, etc. The size and showiness of the mausoleums are in proportion to the stations they held in life when alive.

I had already visited the cemetery. She fairly summed up my impression of the place when she said, "Couldn't they have found a better way of spending that money?" Then she added, "What do you think of Eva Peron's tomb?"

"Too small for her ego," I said. "Her ego deserved something as awe-inspiring as the Taj Mahal. And how presumptuous of her to expect us to cry for her!" I was alluding to the "Don't cry for me" epitaph on Eva Peron's tomb.

She burst into a big laugh and said, "I also had similar reaction when I read the epitaph."

By then, my turn came to approach the reservation desk. I was disappointed to learn that for every deviation from the original booking, I would have to pay 100 U.S. dollars extra. I gave up the idea of extending my stay. For a person traveling on a shoe-string budget, 100 dollars is not a negligible amount. The wonderful conversation I had with the fine Argentine lady helped me easily forget the disappointment at not being able to extend my stay in Buenos Aires.

After I left the reservation counter, I waited until she finished her work. I wanted to continue talking with her. I told her so and invited her to coffee, pointing to the McDonald's around the corner.

She said she had to rush to a job interview. She had lost her job as a chemist a few days earlier. "My husband is still employed. So we don't starve," she said.

But before rushing off, she managed to find just enough time to launch a tirade against McDonald's: "Did you see the invasion of McDonald's in this country? The beef the McDonald's sells is an insult to Argentina. We have the best beef in the world."

She was exaggerating only slightly: Argentina is known for its high-quality beef and Argentines for their "compulsive consumption" of it. The quote is from the late R.W. Apple Jr., who was an editor at *The New York Times*. His food reviews from around the world, which frequently appeared in *The Times*, were as delectable as the foods he reviewed. According to Mr. Apple, an average Argentine's annual consumption of beef was about 130 pounds, more than twice that of an average American.

A Cow-Eating Hindu

My new Argentine friend told me not to leave the country before tasting the Argentine barbecued steak. "It's world-famous and it's genuine steak," she said, placing her right palm on the right side of her waist to indicate where the meat for the steak came from.

Suddenly, she fell silent and looked upset. After a few seconds, she continued, with an expression of guilt on her face. "I am very sorry," she said. "It's beef. Please forgive me. Aren't you a Hindu? I know the cow is supposed to be sacred for Hindus. Please, I didn't mean to offend you."

The profusion of apology and expression of guilt made me say to myself that the cow-worshipers among my Hindu brethren had done a wonderful job. I placed my hands on her shoulders, looked straight into her eyes, and said: "You are looking at a cow-eating Hindu."

She broke into a big smile. I thanked her for the "wonderful conversation" and said good-bye.

Since that day, she has been the second Argentine that comes to my mind whenever I think and read about Argentina. The exalted first place is still held by Gabriella Sabatini, the tennis star of the 1980s. The only thing about her that briefly brought her down from the pedestal on which I had placed her was the grunt she let out every time she served the ball. But then, there are those who say that the grunt, if anything, enhanced her sex appeal.

3

Brahma and Laxmi Reincarnate in Brazil?

Even as a teenager living in India I used to fantasize about visiting Rio de Janeiro. Years later, when I moved to New York, the fantasy got rekindled. It happened when I heard the late Australian singer Peter Allen's famous song, "When my baby flies with me I go to Rio de Janeiro...." At long last, in November 2001, I was able to live that fantasy – of course, with no baby flying with me.

I landed in Rio de Janeiro on a hot and humid evening. It being late spring in that part of the world, I was not expecting that kind of weather. I am not complaining, just making a statement. A person born and brought up in the southern Indian state of Kerala shouldn't be complaining about the hot and humid weather in any part of the world. Moreover, when the beauty of the world-famous Copacabana Beach beckons, complaining about the weather is the last thing one would want to do. Copacabana was just two blocks away from the hotel I checked into.

Though tired, sitting inside the hotel room and idling away the evening, when tourists from all over the world were reveling on the beach a few yards away, was not something I would consider even for a minute. I went out.

The streets were crowded. People looked jolly and happy. The light rain that had been falling for some time failed to keep them indoors. Nor did it dampen their spirits. Most of them were either on their way to the beach or returning from it. Some of the women were fresh from their swim, still in their two-piece swimwear. The rain made the contours of the parts of their body, which the two pieces were supposed to hide, very pronounced. The spectacle was quite an eyeful.

In a few minutes, I was on Copacabana Beach. I walked on the beach as long as my tired feet could drag me, watching swimmers, sunbathers and those frolicking around. I also threw an occasional glance at young couples rolling on the sand and making love.

How Rio de Janeiro Got Its Name

Copacabana extends to Ipanema in a curve. A small piece of land jutting out into the sea separates the two beaches. The body of water in the curve forms a small bay. When Portuguese explorers spotted the bay on January 1, 1502, they mistook it for the mouth of a river. Because it happened in the month of January, they called it Rio de Janeiro, meaning the River of January.

The city that was built around the bay later also took the same name. In time, Rio de Janeiro became the capital of Brazil. It remained so until 1960, the year in which the capital was moved to the newly-built Brasilia. But Rio de Janeiro continued to be the cultural capital of the country. It has enjoyed that status to this day.

By the time I reached Ipanema, I was completely exhausted. I sat on a bench and started musing. When it became dark and the beach started wearing a deserted look, I headed for another part of the city.

On the way, I walked into a convenience store to pick up a bottle of water. The store owner didn't speak a word of English. But I could see that he was anxious to say something to me. And I knew that it had nothing to do with the price of the bottled water I had just picked up. By the time I paid it, he found a way of getting over the language barrier. "Mahatma Gandhi, Indira Gandhi," he said and gave me a handshake.

But for my ignorance of the Portuguese language, I would have convinced him that the latter, though she shared a last name with the former, was a disgrace to him. Through gestures and a "yes" I let him know that he correctly identified my ethnicity. I knew that was what he meant by invoking those two well-known Indian names.

My next stop was at a restaurant. I was happy to see that the food there was served buffet-style and paid for by weight. I could pick what I saw and be sure of what I was eating. No waitress would have to punish herself trying to figure out what I was ordering. (At this particular restaurant, I saw only waitresses, no waiters.)

Ravi Shankar and Kama Sutra

I had just started enjoying the food and the ambience, when I noticed a couple sitting at two tables away staring at me – in an admiring sort of way – and saying something. I smiled at them, and they smiled back. After a few more minutes of staring and smiling, the man came up to me and handed a napkin on which he had written, "Ravi Shankar, very good." I nodded in agreement. That the Indian sitar maestro was popular even among ordinary South Americans made me very happy.

He sat by my side. Soon, his partner also joined us. Both appeared to be in their twenties, and both spoke a few words of English. But the expressions on their faces spoke more than words did. They conveyed, or I thought they did, that they admired India and things Indian very much. We spent a happy one hour together – with laughs, gestures and signs making up for our shortcomings in language. When I was about to leave, the man said, "Kama Sutra, good." That made his girlfriend burst into a loud laugh, inviting the attention of those sitting at nearby tables.

How did I know that she was his girlfriend? Soon after they had come and sat at my table, the man had introduced her to me as his wife. She immediately corrected him: "No, girlfriend."

Maybe there was a message in it for me. But I was too tired to hang around and explore. Moreover, I was booked to go on a conducted tour of the city the next morning.

•

I was on my way to the Sugar Loaf Mountain, a great tourist attraction in Rio de Janeiro. As the tour bus passed by a row of shops, a signboard in front of one of them caught my attention. It had the word Laxmi on it, written in bold letters.

Laxmi, in Hindu mythology, is the goddess of wealth. "Could it be a store selling antiques from India?" "Is it an outlet for some import-export business dealing in Indian goods?" "Is it the office of a company owned by an Indian?" Thoughts like these crossed my mind in rapid succession.

I also thought about other possibilities, like: "Is it a makeshift temple where local Hindus worship?" That seemed remote. The only Indian I had met until then was not a Hindu. He was a Catholic from Goa, living in New York. He had come to Rio de Janeiro to fight a court battle to gain custody of his five-year-old daughter from his estranged Brazilian wife. They had met and married in New York. She had left New York and relocated to her native Rio, taking their only child with her, when he was away in India on a business trip. According to him, she was abusive and alcoholic. He didn't want his daughter to be raised by her.

My next thought was: "Could it be a store doubling as a temple now and then?" I had heard about a garage in New York doubling as a church on Sundays. Some newly arrived Indian immigrants belonging to an out-of-the-mainstream Christian denomination decided that they would feel comfortable only if they congregated separately and communicated with God in their native language, in this case Malayalam. Until they raised enough money to build their own church, they decided to conduct the Sunday mass in a garage. They knew God wouldn't have any problem with that. Wasn't Jesus born in a manger?

The debate in my mind over the word Laxmi on the signboard ended when our bus stopped in front of a cable car. "The cable car will take you to the top of Sugar Loaf," the tour guide announced.

The tour ended in the evening and the tour bus brought me back to my hotel. The "Laxmi" on the signboard continued to intrigue me all night. To satisfy my curiosity, I returned to the place the next morning – only to learn to my utter disappointment that it had nothing to do with goddess Laxmi. Nor had it anything to do with Hinduism, India or Indians. The place was a barbershop. How did a barbershop in Brazil get a Hindu goddess's name? I went in to find out.

There were three employees there, and not a single customer. They were sitting on the swivel chairs meant for customers. Two of them were talking with each other and the third one was half asleep. As I walked in, their faces lit up. Maybe they thought that they got the first customer of the day. There was no reason why they should think otherwise. How often does a person walk into a barbershop with a spiritual question?

The three barbers, like many Brazilians I met, could pass for my compatriots. So I asked them whether they were from India. They spoke a little English, adequate enough to understand my question. No, they were not from India.

How did their shop get the name Laxmi? They didn't know. Only their boss would know, they said. And the boss was not in town that day. He had gone to Sao Paulo to visit his family. I came out disappointed. But I did pray as I came out: "May Laxmi, the goddess of wealth, shower her blessings on this place!" It badly needed blessings from Laxmi.

The Seeker of Universal Truth

Two days later, I had a similar experience – the experience of being elated first at the sight of a Hindu holy name in the unlikeliest of places, only to be disappointed later. It happened on Rua Baratas Ribeiro, a busy street near my hotel. I was on a stroll, walking aimlessly, without paying attention to anything. Suddenly, when I saw the word Brahma staring at me from a faraway billboard, it aroused my curiosity.

Brahma, along with the other two of the sacred triad, enjoys an exalted position in the Hindu pantheon. The other two are Vishnu and Shiva. To the believers among Hindus, Brahma is the Creator, Vishnu the Preserver and Shiva the Destroyer. "What is Brahma doing in Brazil?" I asked myself and walked fast towards the billboard. As I came closer, it became clear that this Brahma had nothing to do with the one the Hindus worship. The billboard was a beer advertisement. The Hindu in me felt let down. Again.

I didn't allow that to bother me for too long, though. It was another hot and humid evening in Rio, and I was feeling very thirsty. I walked into a nearby bar and asked the waitress what the most popular Brazilian beer was.

"Brahma," she said, without a moment's pause.

"Fill it to the rim," I said, borrowing the words from a popular 1970s' coffee advertisement in the U.S.

The gusto with which I said it attracted the attention of a couple sitting next to me at the bar. "You seem to be so excited," the man said. "Do you want to tell us what it's about?"

"With pleasure," I told them. "You see, Mahatma Gandhi once said that in front of a hungry man, God should appear in the form of bread. In front of this thirsty Hindu, God has appeared in the form of beer. I am blessed!"

Pointing to the word Brahma on the bottle, I gave them a brief talk on Hinduism. The talk, as I realized later, was unnecessary in the case of this couple. They had just finished their master's degree in philosophy at the University of London. Both had taken a couple of courses in Hinduism. "But Brahma reincarnating in the form of beer? That adds a whole new chapter to Hindu mythology," the man said.

"Congratulations on your invaluable contribution," his girlfriend added.

"Three cheers for Brahma!" I said, raising my glass. Both of them laughed.

The couple had met at the university and fallen in love. As I was getting ready to leave, they thanked me for the "interesting evening."

"The beauty of being a Hindu," I told them, "is that you are at liberty to laugh at, and with, all the gods and goddesses in your religion. You can even reject them all and still be a Hindu. The Universal Truth you are seeking has no gender or form."

4

How Portugal Failed to Colonize Calicut: My Chat with a Brazilian

It was a pleasant evening, and I was on a leisurely walk on Copacabana Beach. To my left was a row of hotels and expensive mansions and, to my right, the Atlantic Ocean. I couldn't help envying those sitting on the balconies of their hotel rooms and enjoying the spectacular view in front of them – over what sort of drink I couldn't tell. "One day, maybe after I win the New York Lotto, I will have a chance to stay in one of those hotels and give myself that luxury," I said to myself.

It took only a few seconds for me to dispel that envy, with this chastening thought: "Did I ever dream while growing up in that remote village in India that one day, I would be taking an evening stroll on the world-famous Copacabana Beach? I should feel blessed." I continued my stroll until it was dark and then headed for my hotel.

Little did I know while heading for the hotel that another excitement was waiting for me there. As I entered the hotel lobby, I saw a group of people chatting. One of them came up to me and introduced himself. He was the owner of the hotel. "Which part of India are you from?" he asked.

"What made you so sure that I am from India?" I asked, elated by the question, of course.

"There is no mistaking of it," he said. "The stamp is there on your face."

"I am impressed," I told him. "I am from Kerala, which is in the southwestern corner of the country."

I could sense the direction the conversation was going to take. My status as a resident of New York had little relevance to it. So I decided not to mention it for the time being.

"I know where Kerala is," he said. "How far is your hometown from Calicut?"

The question took me by surprise. I was not expecting it from a hotel owner in Brazil. He gave me a warm handshake, as if I had delivered him a gift, when I told him that Calicut was only a few miles away from my hometown. I also told him that Calicut would always have a special place in my heart. I had my undergraduate education at a famous college there. "By the way," I added, "the name of the city has officially been changed to Kozhikode, which was its original name."

Not wanting to be out of step with other developing countries, cities and states in India have lately been restoring their original names, which had been changed by colonial powers during their rule. They did it because they couldn't pronounce most Indian place names. In restoring the old names, Indian leaders have often taken their nationalistic (parochial?) zeal to ridiculous levels. Bombay is now called Mumbai, Calcutta has become Kolkata, Madras has become Chennai and so on. The Brazilian thanked me for the update and made a few futile attempts to pronounce Kozhikode correctly.

"Don't feel bad," I told him, "Even non-Malayalee Indians have difficulty pronouncing it correctly. A Malayalee, by the way, is one who speaks Malayalam and Malayalam is the language of Kerala. We can go into all that some other time. First tell me where your interest in Calicut comes from."

Cabral Left for Calicut, but Ended Up in Brazil

It came from his keen interest in history. Being a history enthusiast myself, I couldn't help taking an instant liking to him. He told me how, by a quirk of circumstance, Calicut got linked to the history of

Portugal's colonization of Brazil. He summed up the link this way: "Do you know that if Cabral had not lost his direction, while on his way to Calicut, Brazil wouldn't have become a Portuguese colony?"

He was being flippant about an important phase in Portugal's overseas expansion. But the question, however, gave an interesting turn to our conversation. I told him how Portugal failed to colonize Calicut.

Pedro Alvarez Cabral led the second Portuguese expedition to Calicut. The first one was led by Vasco da Gama who had reached Calicut on May 27, 1498. As a mission whose goal was "to seek Christians and spices," to quote Vasco da Gama himself, it was a failure. The Arabs, who controlled the entire Indian Ocean trade at the time and who had a monopoly over the spice trade of Calicut, placed all sorts of obstacles on the Portuguese path. With a view to overcoming those obstacles, the Portuguese armed their second expedition formidably and put it under the command of Cabral, an able navigator.

With 13 ships and 1,200 "boldest and most famous seamen of the century" on board, Cabral left Lisbon for Calicut on March 9, 1500. Unfortunately, he did not have a smooth sail. On April 22, he found himself on the coast of Brazil.

There are two versions to how it happened. One goes like this: Anxious to avoid the calm of the west coast of Africa that had considerably slowed the voyage of his predecessor, Cabral went in a decidedly southwestern direction. He realized his mistake only when he spotted a land that did not fit the description of Calicut. The new land he spotted later came to be called Brazil.

The second version is that, before he could veer his fleet around the Cape of Good Hope, a storm drove it off, all the way to the coast of Brazil. More historians have found this version plausible, mainly because of the recurrence of storms in that region. It was one such storm that drove Bartholomeu Dias's expedition around the southern tip of Africa, in January 1488. For that reason, Dias decided to call it the Cape of Storms. King John II of Portugal later renamed it the

Cape of Good Hope, because of the hope it offered of finding a sea route to the East.

If it was a storm that accidentally took Dias around the tip of Africa and paved the way for the epochal discovery of the sea route from Europe to the East, another storm 12 years later, not far from the same place, drove the Portuguese fleet destined for the East away from its chosen path! It is an irony of fate that one of the ships on Cabral's fleet that were destroyed by the storm was commanded by the same Bartholomeu Dias.

Be that as it may, the serendipitous discovery of Brazil by the Portuguese, on April 22, 1500, proved to be a boon for their king back home. On behalf of King Manuel, Cabral took possession of the new land by erecting a cross and holding a religious service. The service was conducted by Father Henrique, a Franciscan priest whom Cabral had brought along.

Cabral resumed his voyage on May 3, 1500, and finally reached Calicut on September 13. (According to some historians the date was August 30.)

The hotel owner to whom I narrated the story was familiar with all facts, including when Cabral left Brazil and continued his voyage for Calicut. He wanted to know what happened after that and why Calicut did not become a Portuguese colony. I filled him in on that to the extent I could draw on my memory:

The first thing Cabral did after reaching Calicut was to send ashore a local fisherman, whom Vasco da Gama had captured during his visit, with a message for the king, the Zamorin. (Zamorin, again, is the anglicized form of the Malayalam word Samoodiri, meaning the lord of the sea.) In the caste-ridden society of the time, sending a fisherman as an envoy to a king was considered an insult. Still, the Zamorin's representatives were courteous enough to negotiate with the Portuguese. After two and a half months' negotiations, the Portuguese were given permission to build a factory at Calicut. (A factory in those days just meant a trading post under the supervision of a factor.)

Arab-Portuguese Rivalry

The favorable treatment given to the Portuguese upset the Arabs. Fearing loss of the monopoly in trade they had been enjoying for centuries, they caused all sorts of problems for the Portuguese and made it impossible for them to function. A frustrated Cabral captured an Arab ship that was loading at the port. In retaliation, the Arabs, with the help of some local men, attacked and destroyed the Portuguese factory. Factor Ayres Correa and 53 of his assistants were killed in the attack.

Cabral struck back. He destroyed 10 large Arab ships and captured 600 sailors from other ships. Though the sailors had nothing to do with the Arab-Portuguese rivalry, Cabral slaughtered them all. After bombarding Calicut with cannon fire for two days, Cabral sailed away. What happened at Calicut had international ramifications. It marked the beginning of a prolonged war the Portuguese waged to gain control of the Indian Ocean trade.

The Brazilian hotelier-cum-history buff was very attentive to my narration. I would have gone on and on, but for the fact that I was getting late and feeling sleepy. Before calling it a night, I told him, "History is full of unanticipated occurrences that permanently altered its course. Your reference to how Brazil accidentally became a Portuguese colony reminds me of what some say about how India became a British colony. According to them, if only the Dutch had not upset the merchants of London by increasing the price of pepper from three shillings to six shillings a pound, there would not have been an East India Company and India would never have become an English colony."

"Oh, oh!" he exclaimed. "That's very interesting. I want to hear more about that part of Indian history. It calls for another session."

He thought for a few moments and then said, "This Saturday, I am taking my wife and a couple of friends out boating. There's a lovely spot out at sea where we go swimming now and then. Why don't you join us? We'll have a good time."

"I don't swim," I told him.

"Doesn't matter," he said. "Come and enjoy the boat ride. Enjoy the beauty of the Brazilian coast from the sea."

"Nothing would I love more," I said and gave him a hug.

I went to bed that night feeling ecstatic.

5

Hunchback and Sugar Loaf: Two Tourist Attractions in Rio de Janeiro

A tourist to Rio de Janeiro doesn't consider his tour complete until he has visited Corcovado and Pão d'Açúcar. The panoramic view of the city one gets from the peaks of these two mountains is indescribable. I visited them on the very second day of my arrival in Brazil.

As the tour bus wound its way up the Corcovado (Hunchback) Mountain, the guide gave a description of the type of people who lived at different levels of the mountain. Actually, his description was unnecessary. One could tell even without it what type of people lived in the hutments of the foothills; what type did in the houses at next levels; and what type in the mansions above them.

Notorious Favelas of Rio

The guide also pointed at a distance to the crime-ridden, drug-infested slum area of the city. Brazilians call it favela. It was the first time that I had a chance to see, though from a distance, the notorious favelas of Rio de Janeiro. Until then, I had only read about them. The entire area is controlled by warlords. Even police and politicians dread to visit the area – unless, of course, they are in cahoots with those warlords. And many of them are. A study conducted by the BBC, which was released around the time I visited the place (November

2001), said that in the preceding 14 years, 4,000 children below the age of 18 had been killed in gun battles in those favelas.

Jackfruits from India and China

We also passed by a lot of jackfruit trees on the way. The guide told us that those trees were originally brought from India and China. I had no problem believing in their Indian origin. They reminded me of my childhood days in Kerala when I used to visit my grandmother's house during summer and other holiday breaks from school. The compound of the house was full of jackfruit trees. The size of some of the fruits that I saw on the Hunchback Mountain would put even Dolly Parton to shame.

Atop the hump of the hunchback is the statue of what they call in Portuguese the Cristo Redentor, meaning Christ the Redeemer. It was built in commemoration of the centennial of Brazil's independence. Brazil declared its independence from Portugal on September 7, 1822. Nine years of arduous work by a team of French artisans headed by sculptor Paul Landowski and 1,145 tons of cement had gone into the making of the statue. Opened to tourists on October 12, 1931, it stands 130 feet tall, on the 2,310-foot-high Corcovado Mountain. Width-wise also, it is enormous. It shows Jesus in an about-to-embrace posture, his hands stretching to a width of 98 feet and 5 inches. The irreverent among Rio residents have a different explanation for that posture. They say Jesus was getting ready to clap for his favorite samba.

For Christians and non-Christians alike, the statue of Christ is reason enough to go to the top of Corcovado. What brings tourists there in droves, however, is the stunningly beautiful view of Rio de Janeiro they get, once they are up there. That view alone makes me want to visit the place again and again.

The next destination of our conducted tour was Pão d'Açúcar. Native Indians had called the 1,296-foot-high granite block pau-nh-acugua (high, pointed peak). The Portuguese, after colonizing Brazil, changed the name to Pão d'Açúcar, meaning sugar loaf. They did it for two reasons: one, it rhymed with the original Indian name; and two, its shape reminded them of the conical loaves in which refined sugar was sold. Though not as tall and lush with trees as Corcovado, the number of tourists it attracts is quite as large. One advantage it has over Corcovado is its location: once on its highest point, one is able to appreciate how mountains covered with luxuriant forests on one side and the Atlantic Ocean on the other enhance the beauty of Rio de Janeiro.

Transportation from the foot of the Sugar Loaf Mountain to its top is by Italian-made cable cars. Riding them is a joy. People prefer to visit the mountain just before sunset, when the granite block and the city below it glisten in the evening sun. They hang around there long after sunset to watch another glistening spectacle: the samba performed by colorfully-costumed dancers at the famous nightclub atop the Sugar Loaf.

After enjoying everything around for some time, we took the cable car back to the foot of the mountain, where our bus was waiting for us. On our way back to the hotel, as we were riding along the beach, I took another look at the petite mountain. "To the Portuguese, it might have looked like a conical loaf," I said to myself. "To me, it looks more like a circumcised penis, when the man is lying down, looking at the ceiling, longing to be with his lover." I dared not say that to our Brazilian tour guide.

6

Yoga on Copacabana, Conducted by a Brazilian Beauty

The one thing I enjoyed the most during the few days I stayed at Rio de Janeiro was the jogging I did on Copacabana Beach every morning. The beauty of the beach certainly had a lot to do with it. And the beauty of scantily-clad women, most of them just basking in the morning sun and some playing volleyball, had something to do with it, too. But what made my mornings the most memorable were the conversations I had with total strangers and some of the spectacles I witnessed, which had nothing to do with the semi-nude women.

One morning, it was a coconut vendor on the beach who caught my attention. I stopped and watched the way he made the hole on the side of the coconut that has its three "eyes" and inserted a straw into the hole, before handing it to the waiting customers. The customers were a young tourist couple. The way he made the hole was too crude to watch for a person familiar with how coconut vendors on the sidewalks of Mumbai do it. The Rio vendor did it by plunging the pointed end of an iron rod into the shell. The Mumbai vendors, most of them lungi-clad Muslims from Kerala, do it with a machete. They do it so artistically, placing the coconut on one of the thighs, that passersby often stop to watch it.

The couple who received the pierced coconut from the vendor threw away the straw and started drinking the milk straight from the coconut. That gave me an excuse to start a conversation with them.

"That's how most people in my home state in India drink it," I told them. "They don't use straws either."

"Which state in India are you talking about?" the woman asked.

When I said "Kerala," she nearly dropped the coconut. "You are from Kerala!" she exclaimed. "I am from Dublin, and I work as a nurse. There are many nurses from Kerala working with me at my hospital. I heard a lot about that place. One day we are going to visit your state."

"It's a place worth visiting," I told her. "Don't be discouraged by the looks of the people from Kerala you have met," I added, pointing at me with my thumb. "They may look ugly. But the place is beautiful. By the way, Kerala gets its name not from the nurses it has exported, but from what you are holding in your hand."

"What do you mean?" she asked.

I explained to her: "In Malayalam, the language of Kerala, the word for coconut is *kera*. Kerala means the land of *kera*. From one end of the state to the other, you can see coconut palms everywhere."

"How interesting," she said. "None of my Kerala friends told me this."

"They will, one day," I told her. "Right now, they are busy making money." I asked her whether she was enjoying her visit to Rio.

"Enjoying is an understatement," she said. "I had been here just three months ago. It was such an unforgettable experience that I was feeling guilty enjoying the trip all by myself. I was impatient to come back and relive the experience with my boyfriend by my side."

She gave a pinch on her boyfriend's cheek before she completed the last sentence. The boyfriend grinned from ear to ear.

"You are a lucky young man," I told him.

Before I took leave of the young Irish couple, I told them not to forget to visit Kovalam Beach if they ever went to Kerala. "It will be another unforgettable experience," I said, and resumed my jogging.

On another morning, it was a different kind of scene that interrupted my jogging. A man was sitting on a bench and videotaping a teenage couple, a few yards away, making love. The couple were all over each other, rolling on the sand, oblivious to their being videotaped. The videographer's friend was sitting next to him, lustily watching the scene. Anyone would be tempted to watch such a scene. The boy's tongue might have reached the girl's esophagus.

Esophagus Kiss

"If you are looking for a title for the video, I have it," I told the videographer. "Call it esophagus kissing. And you must preserve the tape for posterity." He accepted my suggestion with a smile and a nod.

When I told him that I lived in New York, he opened up. "This is November," he said. "This is the third time I am visiting this place since September 11. The place helps me get over the trauma I suffered on that day."

On that day, when a plane piloted by terrorists ran into the World Trade Center in New York, he was at work, at his Morgan Stanley office in Tower One. He was one of those who miraculously survived while many of his co-workers perished in the inferno the World Trade Center turned into. Since then, he had been on disability leave. His disability allowances would continue until his therapist certified him fit to go back to work.

"Since September 11, I have been enjoying every moment of my life with a vengeance," he said. From the way he was savoring the scene on Copacabana, I could tell he was.

On yet another morning, I stopped my jogging to watch a karate class. The class was conducted by a Brazilian, not an Oriental as one would expect. It had 20 students, men and women, young and old, some very old. The very old, I noticed, were of Japanese and Chinese descent. Their dedication and concentration would make any jogger stop and watch. I was intently watching their performance when another jogger stopped and walked toward me. He was bare-chested, might be in his sixties. "Don't you have such things in your country?" he asked me, smilingly.

"Which country?" I said, also smilingly.

"India, of course," he said, "there is no mistaking of it."

A native of Germany, he had been living in Rio de Janeiro for well over a decade. He had been to India several times, he said, and gave me a long list of the places he had visited. "I loved the Pink City," he said.

I told him, shamefacedly, that I hadn't seen as much of India as he did. "The Pink City is one of the places I always wanted to visit," I said, "but haven't got down to doing it yet."

The Pink City is the nickname given to Jaipur, the capital of Rajasthan, one of the states in India. It was a princely state until the country gained independence from Britain, in 1947. Jaipur was founded in 1727 by the state's then-ruler, Maharaja Jai Singh II. It got the nickname, the Pink City, because of the pink color of most of its buildings. A pink wash periodically given to those buildings still preserves that color. The maharaja himself planned and oversaw the building of the city. Jaipur literally means the city of victory, but it got its name from the man who founded it, Jai.

After sharing a bit of history of the city with the German, I told him I was originally from Kerala, "now living in New York."

"Oh, Kerala is one of the places I always wanted to visit but never got down to doing it," he said, mimicking what I had said vis-à-vis Jaipur. But he said it without an iota of sarcasm, and I liked it. We chatted for some more time, exchanged our addresses and went our separate ways.

A Brazilian Fan of Indian Chess Champion

On the following day, I had a more enjoyable conversation with another total stranger, another elderly jogger. He looked back while overtaking me and shouted, "I am sure you can do faster than that."

I laughed. He slowed down to keep pace with me. I knew he wanted to talk with me. "Do you know Vishwanathan Anand?" he asked.

"I will answer that question in a minute," I said. "But before I do, please answer this question: How can you be so sure that I am not a Bangladeshi or a Pakistani?"

"That would have been my third and fourth guesses, not even the second," he replied. "My second guess would put you in Sri Lanka."

"I am really impressed," I told him.

He was a widely-travelled Brazilian and an avid chess player. He said he had participated in many international chess tournaments and played against many world champions, including Kasparov and Karpov. "I always lose to these guys in the first round itself," he added. "But that doesn't bother me. What bothers me is that I never had a chance to play against this child prodigy from India, Vishwanathan Anand. I hope it happens one day before I die."

"I hope so, too," I told him. "And I pray to God that it happens soon."

I really wanted it to happen soon. Vishwanathan Anand earned his reputation as a child prodigy in the world of chess when he started winning major titles at the age of 15. Though not a child anymore (he was born in 1969), I knew he would be around to enjoy many more decades of fame. The endearing Brazilian I had just met appeared to be in his late sixties or early seventies. That was the reason behind my prayer that his wish to play against the Indian chess champion be answered soon.

•

I had many heart-warming experiences like these during my sojourn at Rio de Janeiro. But the one experience I will cherish forever came on the last day. As usual, the day began with my morning jog. It came to a sudden stop when I saw a group of people practicing yoga on the beach. "India meets Brazil on the sands of Copacabana," I said to myself and watched the scene with pride and admiration.

It was an unusually bright day. The yoga students and their young, attractive teacher were in the lotus position, in deep meditation. The morning Brazilian sun that fell on their faces made them look blissful.

I cursed myself, again, for not having my camera with me when I needed it the most. This was not the first time during my travels around the world that I found myself without my camera when presented with a rare photo opportunity.

According to the brochure handed out by an aide to the yoga teacher, the beach session was conducted by Uni-Yoga, a private yoga school with branches all over Rio de Janeiro.

When the teacher and her disciples were still in meditation, I engaged the aide, who spoke a little English, in a brief conversation. He told me his name, which sounded like Iago. I asked him whether the yoga teacher was from India. (She looked strikingly Indian. Could pass for a pretty Maharashtrian.) He said no. She was Brazilian-Indian, the local variant of American-Indians.

Then he asked me whether I was from India. "Your face shows it," he said, when I told him yes.

"What is your name?" he asked.

I said it, of course, with my usual words of caution: "It is too long. You won't be able to pronounce it."

I was to learn in a few seconds that those cautionary words, usually reserved for foreigners, were not necessary in the case of this foreigner. I had to say my name only once, and he repeated it after me, with the right emphasis on each syllable: "Pra bha ka ran."

With the next question, he not only struck me as a person of intellectual curiosity, but also endeared himself to me: "What does your name mean?"

Pointing to the sun, I said: "It means him."

"Oh, you are Surya!" he exclaimed, using the Sanskrit word for the sun.

That nearly floored me. I felt ashamed of myself for having underestimated him. I apologized. He dismissed my apology with a childlike smile.

By then, the class had come out of the meditative posture. The aide rushed to the yoga teacher and said something. When the teacher looked at me, I figured that what he said was about me. From the admiring way she looked at me confirmed to me that what he said about me was something good.

Suddenly, I started getting nervous. "What, if the teacher thinks that being Indian, I may know a lot about yoga? What, if she thinks that it would be a treat for her students if an Indian demonstrated a few yogic postures to them? What, if she requests me to do it?" Thoughts like these crossed my mind in rapid succession.

Not wanting to embarrass me, India and that venerable discipline called yoga, I waved good-bye to the teacher and her aide and resumed my jogging.

Shortcut to Nirvana

More thoughts crossed my mind as I ran: "Do the yoga teacher and her aide know that this Indian knew very little yoga and that what little he knew was self-taught? More important, do they know that long ago, this Indian had found a shortcut to nirvana, which is three pegs of whiskey?"

I ran faster. But I made sure that my feet were firmly on the ground and that my head was far below the clouds. The young Brazilian aide to the yoga teacher had taught me the importance of that.

7

Picture of a Cow on a Beijing Billboard Confuses a Hindu

It was April 2002. I was on a 10-day tour of China, as part of a nine-member group from the United States. (Correction: Actually, there were 10 members in the group. In hindsight, it is wrong for me to count Walter out, simply because he happened to stay behind in the hotel room most of the time. He used a walker to get around. The only reason why he decided to come on this tour was that his wife Dorothy, who was able to get around without a walker, wouldn't travel alone. Having satisfied their wanderlust together all their married life, they didn't want to make this trip an exception. Both were in their late seventies. Whenever I saw them together, they were holding hands. Walter also sang now and then. And he sang beautifully. "If they are this romantic at this stage in life, what a wonderful time they might have had in their courting days!" I remember telling others in the tour group.)

As we came out of the Beijing airport terminal, I noisily inhaled the air, drawing the attention of others in the group. I told them, when they looked at me amusedly, that I was doing in style my first smelling of China. They laughed. I also told them that it was my way of proclaiming to the world that a dream I had been nurturing since childhood – the dream of being in the mythical land of China one day – had at long last materialized. The thrill I felt was oozing out of every pore in my body.

I continued to feel that thrill all through the bus ride from the airport to the hotel, where we would be staying the next two days. The pleasant disposition of the Chinese tour guide, who received us at the airport, made me forget the tedium of the 12-hour flight from Los Angeles to Beijing. She was pretty, in her twenties, and always had a winning smile. Before we reached the hotel, she let it be known to us that she was married.

"I get the message," I told her. "But couldn't you have waited at least until this tour was over?" She blushed.

"Um, you are quite a player, eh," Phoebe, another member of the tour group, who was sitting next to me on the bus, said, with a nudge.

After a good night's sleep, I woke up and looked out of the window of my hotel room. The bright morning sun had already lit up the tree-lined street outside. "Ideal for a morning walk," I said to myself and got out of the room.

Spring Flowers in Full Bloom

It was spring in Beijing and the air was crisp. Spring flowers were in full bloom all around. I once again saw the City Flowers and the City Trees of Beijing, which our tour guide had introduced us to during our bus ride from the airport. The Chinese rose and chrysanthemum are the declared City Flowers of Beijing, and the City Trees are the Scholar Tree and the pine tree.

A casual look at other morning strollers made me aware that I was the only Indian on the street. I became more conscious of it when some of the passersby, all of whom looked Chinese, stared at me. But the stares in no way diminished the joy and excitement I felt on what was my first morning, and first morning walk, in China.

Suddenly, a huge billboard at a distance caught my attention. Embossed on it was the picture of a large cow. The cow aroused my curiosity. "Could it be a pointer to a Hindu temple below?" "Did Hare Krishna people come and set up a temple in Beijing also?" (Their temples are always dedicated to Lord Krishna; and in their minds, and in Hindu mythology, Krishna and the cow are inseparable.) "Is the billboard an advertisement for a dairy farm?" Questions like these arose in my mind as I walked toward the billboard.

I was still at a distance, not in a position to determine what the building below the billboard housed. My curiosity gave way to confusion when I saw a group of men and women, who had just alighted from a tour bus that stopped near the building, walk toward it. From the way most of them dressed, one could tell they were Muslims. Women wore scarves and flowing outer garments. Most men wore tunics, and some had long beard. It is unusual for Muslims to visit a Hindu temple, unless the temple is also a monument of world renown. The guidebook on Beijing that I was carrying had no mention of such a thing. So there was not even a remote possibility of the building being a Hindu temple.

"In what way could these Muslim tourists be attracted to that beautiful cow on the billboard?" I asked myself. I didn't have to wait for long to get the answer. In a minute or so, I found myself standing in front of a restaurant. The billboard with the picture of a cow on it was a display ad of the restaurant below it. The cow in the ad was supposed to mean that it was on the restaurant's menu. The restaurant's name was written, in glittering letters, just below the cow's picture: Xin Jiang Muslim Restaurant. I felt disappointed, again, that I didn't have my camera with me.

Looking at the picture of the fat, beautiful cow, I couldn't help asking myself: "Who in the world would think that a cow this beautiful would end up on a plate in a restaurant?" "But then," I countered it with another question, "how on earth can a cow-eater like me say such a thing?"

The question and counter-question represent the rare moments of conflict in my life – between the Hindu that I was born and brought up as and the cow-eating Hindu that I later became. Every time the conflict arises, I resolve it this way: "A remarkable thing about Hinduism is that its tent is big enough to accommodate both cow-worshipers and cow-eaters."

8

Capitalism Comes to
Mao's Mausoleum

Our 10-day tour of China officially began in Beijing on a beautiful April morning, in the year 2002. Our first destination was the world-famous Tiananmen Square.

All the roads our tour bus wended its way through were crowded, mostly with bicyclists. There were rows and rows of them, at times taking up the entire width of the road, making it difficult for motorists to overtake them. Eight million bicycles and 1.3 million automobiles, which 14 million Beijingers use, were jostling for space in the morning rush hour. It was quite a spectacle.

Tiananmen Square was a good half-hour ride from our hotel. But I was already there, mentally. The rich history of the square was only part of the reason for it. *Tiananmen* in Chinese means the Gate to Heavenly Peace. It was also the gate to the Forbidden City, which was the seat of imperial power in China from 1368 to 1911. During this long five and a half centuries, the country was ruled by emperors belonging to the Ming and Qing Dynasties, in that order.

It was at the gate of the Forbidden City that Mao Zedong proclaimed the People's Republic of China, on October 1, 1949. Tiananmen Square was much smaller in size, when it was the courtyard of the imperial palace, than it is today. After the Communists came to power in 1949, they tore down most of the buildings around the courtyard that were used by imperial ministries. They expanded the courtyard into the sprawling Tiananmen Square that we see today. Today, it is large enough to accommodate 60 soccer fields. During the Cultural Revolution (1966-76), up to a million people used to parade through the square on ceremonial occasions, with a proud Mao Zedong on the review stand. When Mao died, in 1976, another million assembled there to pay him their last respects.

All those details about Tiananmen Square were impressive indeed. But my preoccupation with it on the morning I was heading for it had nothing to do with those details. It had to do with what happened there in 1989. In the spring of that year, the place was the nerve center of a pro-democracy movement in China. The movement that started in Beijing, in April, quickly spread to other major cities of the country. Tiananmen Square was the scene of daily demonstrations by students, demanding democracy and freedom.

The immediate incentive for the demonstrations was a visit by Mikhail Gorbachev, then head of state of the Soviet Union. The Chinese students had already been inspired by the reformation of the Soviet Communist system, which Gorbachev had initiated through what were known as *perestroika* (restructuring) and *glasnost* (openness). The Chinese longed for similar reforms in their country's governing system. Quite coincidentally, the Gorbachev visit also became instrumental in the Tiananmen Square demonstrations' being broadcast live to the whole world. The world media had descended on Beijing to cover the visit.

The Massacre of Demonstrators

But the activities in the square ended abruptly on the night of June 3, when the army moved in and massacred hundreds of unarmed demonstrators and injured thousands of them. According to a report, by Nicholas D. Kristof, that appeared in *The New York Times* of June 21, 1989, "The true number of deaths will probably never be known, and it is possible that thousands of people were killed without leaving evidence behind. But based on the evidence that is now available, it seems plausible that about a dozen soldiers and policemen were killed, along with 400 to 800 civilians."

At the time, Mr. Kristof was the Beijing bureau chief of *The Times*. He goes on to say in the same report: "...many people suspect that troops burned the bodies of many citizens to destroy the evidence of the killings. After soldiers sealed Tiananmen Square about dawn that day, a large bonfire could be seen coming from the square. While it may have been the tents and other remnants of the students' encampment on the square, some fear it was also used to cremate the students' bodies."

Of those who survived, thousands were arrested and charged with "counterrevolutionary" crimes. Most of them have served, and many are still serving, prison terms. Some were executed.

Thirteen years later, I was on my way to the scene of the tragedy. I couldn't contain my anxiety. What I watched on television on that infamous June night in 1989 came back to mind: soldiers firing into the crowd; soldiers clubbing demonstrators until they collapsed; and, the most vivid of all, a courageous young man defiantly standing in front of an advancing column of army tanks, carrying a bag of food for soldiers. The courage he displayed had captured the imagination of the whole world.

Thoughts about him and those who sacrificed their lives in their efforts to bring democratic change in China had taken me to a different world, when an announcement from our tour guide brought me down to earth. We were already in Tiananmen Square, the guide said.

Hawkers in Tiananmen Square

The square's storied past suddenly disappeared from my mind when a crowd of hawkers swarmed us as we came out of the bus. They were young men and women from nearby villages who made a living peddling their wares among tourists. The crude and aggressive way they did it would put their counterparts in any capitalist country to shame. A few yards away from the pushy, noisy hawkers was the famous Mao Mausoleum. The embalmed body of Mao, the father of Communist China, was lying in state inside the mausoleum.

China's rapid growth in the capitalist world market may owe nothing to the Communist ideals that Mao preached. But it owes a great deal to his memory. Outside the mausoleum was a bazaar selling Mao memorabilia – Mao busts, bags, badges, and musical lighters playing short renditions of "The East Is Red." It also sold key rings, thermometers, face towels, handkerchiefs, address books, and cartons of cigarettes. Mao – in case anyone wonders why cigarette was sold as part of his memorabilia – was a chain-smoker. About the commercialization of Mao's name, a commentator has this to say: "Mao might have ruined the Chinese economy, but sales of Mao memorabilia are certainly giving the free market a boost these days."

The hawkers continued to pester us. They shoved their merchandise in our hands and shouted: "Five dollars," "Ten dollars," "Eight dollars." The price was what they fancied at that moment. But there was no fancying about the currency in which they wanted the transaction conducted. It was the Almighty American Dollar, not the Chinese yuan. They wouldn't take no for an answer. They kept insisting that we quote our price if we didn't like what they were asking.

Repeating "How much, how much," they followed us all the way up to the gate of the Forbidden City. There they stopped, not because of any fear of Mao, whose huge portrait overlooking Tiananmen Square was hung over the gate. They stopped because they wouldn't be allowed inside the gate unless they paid the entrance fee.

The Forbidden City

The Forbidden City is called so because, until 1911, entry into it was forbidden to all, except those who were on imperial business. Today, the Chinese government touts it as a great tourist site and prefers to call it the Imperial Palace or the Palace Museum.

Once inside the Forbidden City, we felt greatly relieved. We were relieved that the hawkers were no longer trailing us. We were also excited to be in an entirely different world – the world of the 24 emperors of the Ming and Qing Dynasties, their eunuchs, their concubines and their superstitions. The pleasure-loving emperors rarely came out of their inner chambers. The business of running the empire was mostly left to their favorite eunuchs.

The architecture of the Forbidden City abounds in symbolism. The dragon was the imperial symbol, red the imperial color and nine the imperial lucky number. The red door of the Gate of Supreme Harmony, the main entrance to the Forbidden City's central courtyard, has nine rows of nine nails. The Forbidden City, we were told, has 9999 rooms. We could think of a few better things to do than visit them all to confirm the number.

But we did visit the most important ones, like the Hall of Supreme Harmony, the Hall of Medium Harmony, the Hall of Preserving Harmony, the Palace of Heavenly Purity, the Hall of Union and Peace, and the Hall of Earthly Peace. Each hall was associated with a particular function of the emperor. For example, it was in the Hall of Preserving Harmony that the emperor held banquets and, during the Qing Dynasty's rule, conducted rigorous civil service tests for appointment to various government positions. The highest scorer in the test also became the son-in-law of the emperor.

We also made it a point to visit the dwelling area of some of the concubines. Their tiny rooms – and the tiny beds, tiny tables and chairs, and tiny shoes – made us wonder how tiny they themselves might have been. "How could such tiny beings satisfy imperial appetites?" I jokingly asked my friends in the group.

After wandering through the Imperial Garden at the northern end of the palace, we came out through the northern gate, the Gate of Divine Prowess. There was nothing divine about what we encountered outside the gate, though. It was very worldly: Another group of aggressive salesmen was waiting there to pounce on us. This group was selling not goods, but a tempting service: a quick massage while we were waiting for our bus. Each masseur was carrying a folded chair. There were no masseuses among them and so the six women in our group were spared the harassment. The masseurs concentrated on the three men. "Sit, sit," they shouted, pointing to the chair, "one dollar, one dollar."

"The price is right," I told my friends, "but not the time and place."

After a few minutes' pestering, they gave up on the two American males and started concentrating on me. Being the only Indian in the group, I might have struck them as an easy target. When the pestering became too much, three women from our group came to my rescue. They formed a protective circle around me and one of them said, "I won't let my husband spend any more money today."

That didn't work either. One of the masseurs found that a small area of my buttocks was still unprotected. He reached for the area with one hand and started massaging it. With the other hand, he opened the chair and placed it close to my rear end. "One dollar, one dollar," he kept shouting, "sit, sit."

Fortunately, our bus arrived before he could force me to sit on the chair. All of us hurriedly got on the bus. I heaved a sigh of relief.

I was the last to enter the bus. "Ladies and gentlemen," I said soon after entering, "democracy might not have come to Communist China, but capitalism has. It has come all the way up to Mao's mausoleum, but in its crudest form."

My friends in the tour group had a good laugh.

9

Capitalist Celebrations in Communist China – That, Too, on May Day

For workers around the world, May 1 is an important day. It is celebrated as May Day with pomp and pageantry. And communist countries, when communism was a major force in international politics, used to add a revolutionary zeal to it. That's something one would naturally expect from the champions of the proletariat.

The origins of May Day had nothing to do with communism or the proletariat, though. They can be traced to pagan Europe, which observed May 1 as a holy day celebrating the first spring planting. Even now, many countries observe it in that tradition. They observe it in celebration of spring. In many countries, it's also a declared holiday.

May Day's association with labor happened centuries after it originated as a holy day. It happened as a result of the prolonged struggle by workers of the United States and Canada, demanding reduction of the workday to eight hours. May 1, 1886, the day they struck work at various industrial centers, was a turning point in that struggle. The nerve center of the struggle was Chicago. There, the police attacked the strikers, killing six of them. Three days later, at a demonstration held in the city's Haymarket Square to protest the killing, a bomb exploded, resulting in the deaths of eight policemen. It has not been resolved to this day whether the bomb was thrown at the police by the workers or by one of police's own agent provocateurs. Eight trade unionists were arrested and, after a perfunctory trial, four of them – Albert Parsons, August Spies, George Engle and Adolph Fischer – were executed.

Communist Co-option of May Day

The foregoing digression is done for a reason. It is done to drive home the point that the working class in capitalist America had sacrificed a lot to make May Day what it is today. The gusto with which the communists have been celebrating it should not make anyone overlook that fact. The communists' association with, if not co-option of, May Day took place at the Paris meeting of the International Working Men's Association (the First International), on May 1, 1889. The meeting passed a resolution, declaring May 1 as a holiday for the international working class. The First International did it in memory of the martyrs of Chicago's Haymarket Square.

Before the disintegration of the Soviet Union, the May Day parade in Moscow's Red Square used to be an annual event that the communists around the world proudly talked about. The leader of the Communist World, which the Soviet Union was at the time, used the day to show off its military might and the superiority of its form of government. The form of government, as professed by the communists, was the dictatorship of the proletariat. In time the world came to know that it was only a show. The dictatorship of the proletariat could not keep up the show for too long. It collapsed under its own weight. With the collapse of the Soviet Union, China became the unchallenged leader of the Communist World, or what was left of it.

I was in Shanghai, China, on May 1, 2002. I woke up in the morning, excited at the prospect of watching May Day celebrations in the only communist country of any clout left in the world. And Shanghai's status as the business capital of that country added to the excitement.

Armed with a camera and lots and lots of films, I stepped out of my hotel on Cao Xi Road, a thoroughfare in Shanghai. I wanted to record for posterity all of the activities associated with May Day.

The first scene that caught my attention was a makeshift stage in front of a huge Kentucky Fried Chicken (KFC) franchise. China, at the time, had more than 600 KFC outlets. McDonald's was fast catching up. "Capitalist penetration in Communist China?" I wondered. Loudspeakers were blaring from different corners of the stage. I could not tell from the distance what it was all about. On a huge billboard behind the stage was the KFC logo – the picture of smiling, goateed Colonel Sanders, the founder of KFC. The picture made me wonder: "Could those guys on the stage be shouting 'Down with imperialists and their running dogs'?"

As I came closer, it became clear that they were not shouting Mao Zedong's favorite slogan. In fact, they were celebrating what Mao would have condemned as something associated with the decadent bourgeois culture. They were conducting a fashion parade.

The background music added to the bourgeois flavor of the event. It was very American. They were playing Whitney Houston's famous song, "The Greatest Love of All." Swaying to the rhythm of "I decided long ago never to walk in anyone's shadow…," young Chinese girls, slim and pretty, ambled onto the stage in all kinds of costumes, nightgowns included. The only communist restriction on this capitalist encroachment was that there was no display of swimsuits. I was disappointed. "Maybe the Chinese needed some more time to get over that restriction," I said to myself. After all, both Whitney Houston songs and capitalism arrived in China pretty late.

Celebration of Cell Phone

On the other side of Cao Xi Road was Hui Jin Department Store. Going by the abundance of goods and by the tasteful way they were displayed, the store could easily rival Macy's, the giant American department store. On the sidewalk in front of the store, another group was celebrating China's successful entry into another area of the capitalist world economy – the area of mobile phones. Tiny children were distributing flyers announcing the arrival in the market of mobile phones manufactured by Lucent Technologies. The

American telecom giant might have suffered enormous losses globally in preceding years. But its operations in China at the time were reported to be lucrative. It had succeeded in cornering a significant part of the country's cell-phone market, which until recently was dominated by Nokia of Finland and Motorola, another American company.

According to Joseph Kahn of *The New York Times*, by the end of 2002, "China had registered more than 200 million mobile-phone users." The flyer-distributing children were wearing T-shirts, with the logo of Lucent Technologies prominently printed on them. "Workers of the world, unite," I was tempted to shout, "you have nothing to lose but your old-fashioned rotary phones!"

Anxious to see an authentic May Day event, I walked, and walked. There was none. Disappointed, I decided to take the subway to People's Square, which was only a few minutes' ride from where I was. "A place named after people may have something celebrating their cause on a day like this," I said to myself while getting on the train.

The area surrounding the station where I got off was once the venue of the Shanghai Racecourse. Now it is occupied by the Shanghai Museum and People's Park. The museum, designed to look like a ding, the ancient Chinese vessel symbolizing power, was built in 1994, at a cost of 570 million yuan (about 83.5 million U.S. dollars). It has an impressive collection of Chinese art and takes one through the pages of China's history.

At People's Park, men and women hang out – some doing nothing; and others making love, taking a nap, gossiping, roller-skating or just daydreaming. All those activities and inactivity were going on when I arrived there, too. In fact, there were more of them, May Day being a holiday in Communist China. But none of them could even remotely be interpreted as celebratory of the working class.

Disappointed, and also tired, I sat on a concrete bench in an isolated part of the park. I asked myself: "Wouldn't Mao be disappointed, too, if he were to visit Shanghai today?"

10

How a Shanghai Neighborhood Got an Indian Name

It was my last day in Shanghai. The group I had been traveling with had already left for the U.S. I had decided to stay back for two more days, hoping to explore more of Shanghai, this time all by myself. I wanted to explore more of the Bund and the areas around it. Some of the travel brochures I browsed tout the Bund as one of the top-ten tourist attractions in Shanghai.

One may wonder how a Chinese neighborhood got an English name, which in turn was derived from Hindi. The word *bund* in Hindi means an embankment built to control the flow of water. The Hindi word had entered the English lexicon long before the British built an embankment along the Huangpu River and developed its muddy shore into a modern waterfront with impressive residential mansions and business houses. The incentive for development came from the flourishing trade, especially the illegal opium trade, they had been conducting in the area for quite some time. The opium trade was conducted mainly through the East India Company.

By the time the newly-developed area in Shanghai came under British control, the East India Company had been in India for nearly two and a half centuries. After 1757, the company, chartered by Queen Elizabeth I of England, on December 31, 1600, to trade with the East, also started ruling parts of India. Thanks to the long interaction between England and India, numerous Indian words, including *bund*, got incorporated in the English language. So much for the etymological origin of the English word bund and the historical origin of the Bund in Shanghai.

Britain got control of the area in 1842. It happened as a result of the Treaty of Nanjing that ended the First Opium War. The treaty, which was imposed on China by Britain, opened Shanghai to Westerners. It virtually ceded three areas of the city to Western powers. Apart from Britain, the other Western powers that benefited from the new opening were France and the United States. The two countries came to possess pieces of Shanghai by virtue of unequal treaties they separately signed with China in 1844 – the Treaty of Whampoa signed by France and the Treaty of Wanghia signed by the U.S. Known as Foreign Concessions, these newly-acquired areas were autonomous settlements and immune from Chinese laws. The Japanese began to arrive in Shanghai only in 1895.

Foreigners Amass Wealth

While Britons and Americans later combined their concessions into what was called the International Settlement, the French kept their concession separate. All foreigners living in Shanghai amassed immense wealth through trading in opium, silk and tea, and also running gambling joints and brothels. In time the Bund earned the nickname "the Wall Street of Shanghai."

The autonomy the Western powers enjoyed over parts of Shanghai came to an end in 1949, the year in which the city, along with the rest of China, came under Communist rule. It was in Shanghai that the Chinese Communist Party was born (in 1921). It was also in Shanghai that Mao Zedong "cast the first stone of the Cultural Revolution." The 1966-'76 Cultural Revolution set China back by several decades. The notorious Gang of Four, which tyrannized the country during that revolution and of which Mao's wife was the kingpin, used Shanghai as its power base.

The Chinese Communists put this once-vibrant commercial and cultural center into a long slumber. It was reawakened only in

1990, when the central government, under the leadership of Deng Xiaoping, decided to pour money into it to revive its vitality.

Though the Bund is no longer a Western enclave, it is still very European in appearance. The waterfront reminded me of the promenades by the Thames in London and by the Seine in Paris. I took a leisurely walk in the Bund, enjoying everything around. I chatted with tourists passing by and waved to those on boats cruising through the Huangpu River. The 71-mile-long river, which flows from the mouth of the Yangtze River to the East China Sea, is known for long and short, day and night, pleasure cruises. I had taken a short night cruise two days earlier.

The night cruise was also an eye-opener for me. It was during that cruise that I realized to what extent capitalism had penetrated Communist China. Billboards and buildings on both sides of the Huangpu River had neon signs advertising products and services of every multinational corporation of repute in the world. The well-lit, colorful riverbanks added to the pleasure of the cruise all right. But it also raised an important question: "Why does China still insist on calling itself Communist?"

Pudong – the Special Economic Zone

Across the river from the Bund is Pudong, the special economic zone of Shanghai. Its Manhattan-like skyline is the outcome of an urban development project undertaken in the 1990s, at a cost equivalent to 40 billion U.S. dollars. Again, it was Deng Xiaoping who quickened the pace of the development. It has been reported that during a 1992 visit to Pudong, Deng chastised city administrators for the slowness of Shanghai's economic growth. If China is the fastest-growing economy in the world today, the credit for it should go to Deng, whom Mao and the Gang of Four had condemned as a "capitalist-roader." In 1966, he was ousted from all positions of power and responsibility.

Once back in power, in 1978, this time as the country's Paramount Leader, the one-time "capitalist-roader" decided to take precisely that road. He did it while keeping the Communist flag still fluttering, though. The result? Flourishing business centers like Pudong began to spring up around the country and Chinese goods began to flood markets around the world. The same Communists who had ridiculed Deng Xiaoping two decades earlier now started singing his praise.

Pudong may boast a Manhattan-like skyline. But the buildings in the area are no match for the graceful colonial mansions of the Bund. Also, the skyscrapers of Pudong have added to the fear, which Shanghai residents have been living with – the fear that their city, which was built on a swamp, is steadily sinking. According to a report, by Jim Yardley, which appeared in the October 14, 2003, edition of *The New York Times*, the city sank about eight feet from 1921 to 1965. In 1965, "officials managed to correct the problem and virtually stop the sinking – for a while." But only for a while. The same *Times* report warned that "the city is again sinking, at roughly a centimeter a year."

The sinking problem did not stop the building activities in Pudong. And it did not in any way diminish the joy I felt while viewing Pudong from the Bund side of the Huangpu River.

11

A Jacket and a Bride for the Price of One: Shopping on Nanjing Road

After spending most part of my last day in China enjoying Pudong and the Bund in Shanghai, I headed for the nearby Nanjing Road (*Nanjing Lu*, in Chinese). All my friends who had been to Shanghai before me, and all travel guides I read, had strongly recommended that I shouldn't leave Shanghai without spending some time on Nanjing Road.

At the entrance to the road from the Bund is the famous Peace Hotel. The hotel has a storied past. Its two wings, straddling Nanjing Road, were two independent, privately-owned hotels – Cathay Hotel, to the north, and Palace Hotel, to the south – before Shanghai and the rest of China came under Communist rule, in 1949. Cathay was opened in 1929. It was part of the Sassoon House, built by Sir Victor Sassoon, a British-Sephardic Jew of Iraqi origin. He had made a fortune in Shanghai, trading in opium and weapons. After the Communist takeover, the hotel became government-owned. It was renamed Peace Hotel in 1956.

The history of Palace Hotel goes back to the 1850s. Built as part of the Palace Building, its original name was Central Hotel. Among Palace Hotel's celebrity occupants was Sun Yat-sen, who stayed there during the 1911 Xinhai Revolution. It may be added that it was the Xinhai Revolution that eventually ended the rule of the Qing Dynasty in China and established the country as a republic.

The hotel also boasts of having hosted the first meeting of the World Anti-Narcotics League, in 1909. It shouldn't surprise anyone that such a meeting was held at Palace Hotel, not the nearby Cathay. It would be inappropriate for a hotel built partly with the money made through illegal opium trade to host an anti-narcotics event. During World War Two, Palace Hotel was occupied by the invading Japanese army. It became part of Peace Hotel in 1965.

The history of Nanjing Road dates back to 1851. At that time, it was called Park Lane. It got the English name because it was part of the International Settlement (discussed in Chapter 10), administered by the British and the Americans. In 1865, the English-speaking administrators renamed it Nanking Road. Nanking is the anglicized form of Nanjing.

The road gets its name from the city of Nanjing. Nanjing became known all over the world, not because it was the capital of China for a long time, but because of the large-scale looting, raping of women and massacre of innocent people that took place in the city in 1937. The atrocities were committed by the invading Japanese army, and have been graphically described in a 1997 book, *The Rape of Nanking*, written by Iris Chang.

Extending all the way from the Bund to Jingian District, Nanjing Road is said to be the longest (more than three miles long) street in Shanghai. With over one million visitors a day, it is also reputed to be the busiest shopping area in the world.

The part of Nanjing Road that is called Nanjing Road East is reserved exclusively for pedestrians. It reminded me of *Calle Florida* (Florida Street) in Buenos Aires, Argentina – with the difference that this one is busier all through the day and most of the night and that it is much longer. Also, while only part of Nanjing Road is reserved for pedestrians, the entire Florida Street is kept that way.

Most of Shanghai's oldest and largest department stores are located on Nanjing Road. There are also small stores, overflowing with merchandise that suits varied tastes and budgets. As I walked along, I could see in some of them glittering arrays of Chinese silk. There were also teeny-weeny stores and kiosk-like outlets selling antiques, handicraft, trinkets, and curios. What was once the hub of European-style restaurants and cafes, Nanjing Road is now a preferred shopping place for the rich and poor alike. Some stores were also overflowing with saleswomen, by which I mean that their numbers were far out of proportion to the quantity of merchandise in them. Salesmen were rare.

Saleswomen Acting as Matchmakers

As I was passing by a ready-made-apparels store, a jacket that was on display on a mannequin caught my attention. Two saleswomen from the store, who might have noticed my more-than-casual interest in the item, came out and grabbed my hands. "Come look, no buy," they said and dragged me into the store.

Before I could say no, they pulled the jacket off the mannequin and put it around my shoulders. Then they pushed me toward a mirror and said, "Look, you good."

One of the women pressed some numbers on a calculator to show me the price. By then, I had decided that I liked the jacket and that I was going to buy it. I told her, using my ten fingers to translate it, how much I was willing to pay. After a few minutes' haggling, we decided on a price, and I bought the jacket. Though they wanted me to pay for it in American dollars, I did it in their own currency – which they proudly call *renminbi*, meaning people's currency.

I was ready to leave the store, but the two saleswomen wouldn't let me. They dragged me to a showcase and pointed to a lady's outfit – a sleeveless blouse and a matching skirt, both made of silk. "This, your wife, good," one of them said.

"I am single," I told them, the index finger of my right hand emphasizing the point.

"Oh, you single! Good."

They had a solution for that problem, too. They escorted me to a corner of the store. Pointing to a young woman sitting at a desk there, one of them said, "She manager. Single. You two good." The manager blushed.

"I am leaving Shanghai tonight," I told them, my gestures and signs supplementing the words. "Marriage next time. I promise."

My promise made both women giggle. The manager giggled, too. All three were twenty-something and good-looking.

I left the store, saying to myself, "A jacket and a bride for the price of one? Not a bad deal."

Looking back, I am happy that I didn't allow myself to be shanghaied by three women, two of them buxom.

12

A Morning Walk by the Mekong; A Restaurant Having My Niece's Name

The Mekong River is 2,700 miles long. It is the twelfth-longest river in the world. Starting from the Tibetan plateau, it flows through or borders on six countries – China, Myanmar, Thailand, Laos, Cambodia, and Vietnam – before emptying into the South China Sea. It's known by a different name in each country it flows through. In terms of biodiversity it provides to the areas it touches, the Mekong is second only to the Amazon River.

I recalled these details when I set out on an early-morning walk during my brief stay in Luang Prabang, Laos, in November 2006. The details also reminded me that, during the short walk I was going to take on Luang Prabang Road overlooking the Mekong River, I would be able to enjoy only a tiny part of the beauty this wonderful river is known for. However, the disappointing thought vanished the moment I got the first glimpse of the river.

It was a pleasant November morning. The sun had just risen, giving a copper-color coating to the surface of the river. The water in the river was churning. It has always been churning in the Luang Prabang area, they say. None has found out why. The lush forest the river snakes through adds to its beauty.

The serenity of the morning was pleasantly disturbed by the occasional chirp of birds and footsteps of joggers. All joggers that I saw were foreigners. I could also tell from the way they responded to my "Good morning" that most of them were from Australia.

"It's quite a treat, eh," I said to one of them. In fact, I was speaking for myself. For a person living in New York City, a morning jog on an empty road that winds its way through wooded areas overlooking a river is, indeed, a rare treat.

"It is," the man replied. Then he waved to me and said, "Good day," in the typical Australian fashion. By which I mean that it sounded "Gudai."

I felt great. "I will be reminiscing this experience for a long time," I thought to myself and continued walking. Little did I know then that what was going to make my morning walk by the Mekong River really memorable was yet to come.

Nisha Indian Restaurant

I might have walked for another five minutes when a sign on the opposite side of the road aroused my curiosity. "Nisha Indian Restaurant," it said, with an arrow pointing to a side street.

In the two days that I had been in Luang Prabang, I had not met a single Indian, let alone see an Indian restaurant. What added to my excitement was that the road-sign indicated not just any Indian restaurant, but one that bore my niece's name. "How did a restaurant in a Laotian town get my niece's name?" I wondered. To find out, I walked in the direction the arrow pointed.

The restaurant was the front of a house in which its owner and his family lived. It was too early for any customer to be around. A man in a lungi, that ubiquitous loincloth most South Indians wear at home, was playing with a little girl on the veranda of the house. His South Indian features were unmistakable, and he could easily pass for a cousin of mine. "He must be the owner," I said to myself.

"Which part of South India are you from?" I asked him, at the risk of sounding presumptuous.

"Pondicherry," he said.

Pondicherry is one of the former French-colonial enclaves in India, about a hundred miles to the south of Chennai. Even after the rest of India gained independence from Britain in 1947, the French and the Portuguese continued to cling to their colonial possessions in the country. The Indian territories under Portuguese control were Goa, Daman and Diu. While the government of independent India, after protracted negotiations, persuaded the French to depart voluntarily, it had to engage in a mini-military operation to get rid of the Portuguese. The French departed in 1954 and the Portuguese were expelled in 1961.

In colonial days, people from one colony could move to another with minimal travel restrictions. Laos was a French colony from 1893 until it declared its independence in 1945. It became completely free of French control in 1954. The Indian restaurateur appeared to be in his late thirties or early forties, not old enough to have left Pondicherry and moved to Laos when both were French colonies.

"How long have you been here?" I asked him.

"Thirteen years," he said.

If I had more time at my disposal – I had to leave Luang Prabang by noon – I would have asked many more questions to satisfy my curiosity. I would have asked questions like how a person from a former French colony in India ended up in a former French colony in Southeast Asia. Those who were well off usually went to Paris and other major cities of France. But I had to ask him the one question that brought me into his restaurant: How did he come up with the name Nisha for his restaurant?

"Oh, Nisha is my daughter," he said, pointing to the girl who was running around the place. She could be about seven or eight years old.

"My niece's name is Nisha, too," I told him.

I had expected him to say something in reply or, at least, smile. He did neither.

I ordered a South Indian breakfast – *dosa, sambaar* and tea. The tea was from Darjeeling, the beautiful hill station in the Indian state of West Bengal, famous for its tea. Darjeeling had no French connection, though.

13

A Humbling Experience in a Laotian Town

It was November 23, 2006. I woke up in the morning feeling sad that I had only a few more hours left to spend in Luang Prabang. The day before, I had been out all day, exploring the town.

Area-wise, it doesn't take one full day to cover the length and breadth of the town, even on foot. But there is something exotic about this lush, little Laotian town, at the confluence of the Mekong and Nam Khan Rivers, which leaves one with a feeling that he hasn't had enough even after taking in its beauty all day.

In an article published in *The New York Times* of March 11, 1990, Nicholas D. Kristof, the paper's Beijing bureau chief at the time and now one of its opinion columnists, describes Luang Prabang as "one of the most authentic windows left on Asia as it used to be."

I wouldn't go that far. Maybe it was so in 1990 when he wrote the article. Since then, it has changed a lot. But it still has a charm of its own, a charm that prompted the United Nations Educational, Scientific and Cultural Organization (UNESCO) to include it in its World Heritage Sites list. Ever since UNESCO bestowed that honor on it in 1995, Luang Prabang has been enjoying the same status as Angkor Wat of Cambodia, the Taj Mahal of India and other World Heritage Sites. And it has also been enjoying a steady influx of tourists.

The place gets its name from *Pra Bang*, meaning little Buddha in Lao. The little Buddha's image, a tad below 33 inches in height and about 119 pounds in weight, was cast in a mixture of gold, silver and bronze. It was cast in Sri Lanka, reportedly in the first century, and taken to Cambodia. It was given to the ruler of Laos in the 15th century when the kingdom came under Cambodian suzerainty.

A gilt bronze copy of Pra Bang now sits in the National Museum in Luang Prabang. The original statue, 90 percent of which is gold, is kept under lock and key in the country's national bank. The statue shows the Buddha standing, with arms raised at the elbows, palms facing forward. This hand gesture, known as the *Abhaya Mudra* (the sign of fearlessness), signifies assurance and protection.

The museum – which was once the royal palace, built by King Sisavang Vong between 1904 and 1909 – is now one of the main tourist attractions in Luang Prabang. Apart from the bronze copy of Pra Bang, it houses the royal throne of the Lan Xang Kingdom and many other regalia and religious treasures.

Women's Status

I couldn't help noticing one thing when I saw the king's and queen's bedrooms in the museum. I am not referring to the difference in size of the rooms. I am referring to the noticeable difference in elegance of the two beds. The king's bed has a headboard and a footboard. The footboard has Erawan, the three-headed elephant, symbolizing the three kingdoms of Laos, carved on it. All these are missing from the queen's bed. Does it have something to do with Theravada Buddhism, the variant of Buddhism practiced in Laos? The thought did cross my mind. Theravada, meaning the Doctrine of the Elders, doesn't give women equal status with men.

However, what I had witnessed while entering the museum was reason enough for me to dispel that thought. It reminded me that the Laotian society has outgrown the religious doctrine that treated women unequally. In front of the statue of Pra Bang, which was only a few feet away from the entrance, I had seen women in blue jeans sitting side by side with men and chanting the famous Buddhist prayer:

Buddham Sharanam Gachhami,
Dharmam Sharanam Gachhami,
Sangham Sharanam Gachhami

Which, in English, means: "I seek refuge in the Buddha, I seek refuge in the Dharma (the teachings), I seek refuge in the Sangha (the community)]."

Progress represented by women's wearing of blue jeans may be dismissed by some as merely cosmetic. But Luang Prabang also has concrete evidence to prove that the progress the women of the place have achieved is more than cosmetic. Most of the restaurants, guesthouses and other businesses in the town are either run by women or owned by them. And at the night market, which the long stretch of the road in front of the museum gets transformed into at sunset, and which is another big draw among tourists, those I saw selling their merchandise were mostly women.

One of those women got into a heated argument with me when I accidentally stepped on, and partially damaged, an antique ashtray she had displayed on the floor. She wouldn't let me go until I compensated her for the damage. She and most other vendors knew as much English as was necessary to conduct business with foreigners – which is another sign of progress.

Apart from Pra Bang, the city has another important association with the Buddha. Legend has it that "the Buddha smiled when he rested here for a day during his travels, prophesying that it would one day be the site of a rich and powerful capital city."

In 1354, it became the capital of Lan Xang Kingdom or the Kingdom of a Million Elephants. The capital moved to Vientiane in 1560. The move was significant only politically, though. Luang Prabang continued to be the cultural capital of Laos. It has remained so till today.

Special Gift to Foreigners

As I had only a few more hours left to savor Luang Prabang, I got out of the guesthouse, where I was staying, very early in the morning. There was another reason for my getting out that early: the owner of the guesthouse had told me the previous night that if I could go to the street corner outside before sunrise, I would be witnessing something very special.

"What is it?" I had asked her.

"Go and see it for yourself. It is Luang Prabang's special gift to foreigners," she had said.

I was not going to miss it for anything in the world. I was out at the street corner at 5:45 in the morning. Two other foreign tourists, who also knew about this "special gift," had already arrived there. They wanted to capture the moment, one of them on his video camera. He told me what we were going to see.

A few women were sitting at the street corner, with baskets and bowls in front of them. They were waiting for Buddhist monks from nearby monasteries, who would soon be coming by to collect what they had in their baskets and bowls. What they had were their offerings – the monks' food for the day, mainly rice.

In Buddhism, giving and receiving alms are considered rituals. Because they are rituals, the givers don't call what they give alms. They call them their offerings to the monks. Buddhist monks don't beg. They accept whatever is offered. It is a common practice among them, especially in Asian countries, to go around the village early in the morning with bowls in hand and collect the devotees' offerings. In Luang Prabang, the devotees go a step further. They go out and meet the monks half-way.

Rows of Orange-Robed Monks

In a few minutes, rows and rows of orange-robed monks, with bowls in hand, began to arrive. The color of the robe the Buddhist monks wear varies from country to country. All the monks I saw in

Luang Prabang wore orange-colored robes. For monks and nuns, robes and bowls are very important. The Buddha had said: "Just as a bird takes its wings with it wherever it flies, so the monk takes his robes and bowl with him wherever he goes."

According to the precepts of Theravada Buddhism, women are not supposed to stand higher than monks. That could be the reason why all women who had come to the street corner with their offerings were seen sitting. Though they were sitting, rather than kneeling as is the Buddhist custom, there was not an iota of immodesty in any one of them.

It was awesome to watch the smiling monks silently arrive, collect in their bowls what the smiling Laotian women offered, and then move on to the next street corner, and thence to the next neighborhood. I knew that any one of them was competent, and some of them qualified, enough to take up any job in this modern world. Any one of them could easily have more material comforts than what the daily offerings of the devotees provided them. But, following in the footsteps of the Buddha, they chose the life of total renunciation and the contentment that came from it.

For a person living in New York, in a 'per-hour society' that measures success in life in terms of the amount of money one makes per hour, it was quite a revelatory experience – a very humbling one.

14

Garbage Dumps and Traffic Jams in the Silicon Valley of India

Bangalore, the capital of the southern Indian state of Karnataka, has made remarkable progress in the area of information technology (IT). There aren't many cities in the world that attract as many outsourced high-tech jobs from the United States and Europe as Bangalore does. The city has deservedly been called the Silicon Valley of India, after the place in the San Francisco Bay Area in the U.S. which pioneered the personal computer and IT revolution. Silicon Valley, it may be added, became the center of the dot-com bubble of the mid-1990s.

Though the bubble has since burst, the valley still retains its status as one of the leading Internet- and computer-related research and development centers in the world. The burst, however, did not affect Bangalore's rapid advancement on the information superhighway – to borrow an expression coined by former U.S. Vice President Al Gore.

The sudden fame has transformed Bangalore from what was once a laid-back city, where Indian civil servants and military personnel belonging to the upper echelon preferred to spend their retirement years, into one of the preferred destinations of travelers from around the world. There is hardly any coffee shop or antique store on Mahatma Gandhi Road and Brigade Road, two favorite tourist haunts, where one doesn't come across foreigners sipping coffee, gossiping or window-shopping.

Many of them are backpackers in their twenties. And all of them seem to be happy. No complaints about the price of the coffee or of any merchandise they buy. For those traveling with euros and U.S. dollars, the prices of goods and services in India should give no cause for complaints. But there are constant complaints among them, though, about the city's crumbling infrastructure, public transportation system and deplorable sanitary condition.

A lot has been written about the problems related to Bangalore's infrastructure. It is to the credit of the city and state governments that both have given top priority to modernizing the infrastructure. Their determination to build a modern metro system* is a major step in that direction. No visitor can fail to notice the construction activities going on all over the city. But the problem is that modernizing the infrastructure built for a 19th-century small town is much more difficult than building a new one suitable for a bustling city of the 21st century. The whole city is densely populated, and no construction activity can be undertaken without causing considerable inconvenience to the public. To make matters worse, there are politicians always at the ready to exploit people's difficulties and turn them into votes, in the following election, against the party in power. So if the work on infrastructure, even the much-trumpeted Namma Metro (our metro) is slow, the party in power is only partly to blame.

Stray Dogs and Stray Cows

The same is the case with the ever-deteriorating sanitary and traffic conditions. The sanitary condition is made worse by people who routinely dump garbage on streets and sidewalks. It hurts the sensibilities of those who love the city to see piles and piles of garbage lying around and stray dogs and stray cows helping themselves to whatever they find edible. Not just stray animals, even human beings often rummage garbage piles – that, too, with their bare hands. They are looking for salvageable objects, so they can make a living selling

---

* *UPDATE: The first phase of the Bangalore metro was inaugurated on October 20, 2011.*

them. Sights like these ill behoove a city that takes pride in being the IT capital of India.

To the extent that it still relies on primitive ways of clearing the garbage and disposing of it, the city administration is to blame. By 'primitive ways' I mean that sanitary workers still use hand-held brooms and clear the garbage with bare hands. People who dump the garbage on streets are equally to blame for this deplorable situation.

Another problem that often makes life miserable, not just for tourists but for the local people also, is the city's perennial traffic jams. They have become very much part of the city life that people have stopped complaining about them. Many Bangaloreans, politicians counted first, campaigned for years to change the city's name to Bengaluru, because that happened to be the name of the place in folklore, fables and stone inscriptions. One wishes that they had spent half as much time campaigning to clean up the filth in the city and improve its steadily deteriorating traffic condition.

City's Name Should Be 'Jamgalore'

An opinion piece that appeared in the May 2, 2009, edition of *The Times of India*, one of India's leading English dailies, says that the city's name should have been changed not to Bengaluru but "Jamgalore." One couldn't agree with the author of the piece more. "In Bangalore," says Jug Suraiya, the author, "people talk of traffic jams. They talk of the traffic jams they got into yesterday, and the ones they will probably get into tomorrow," while "still stuck in day before yesterday's jam."

There are only a few roads in the city which have traffic lights and sidewalks. Motorists often ignore 'stop' signs, especially when there are no traffic police around. Their disregard for traffic rules causes not just traffic jams but accidents, too. The IT capital of India has also become the accident capital of India. The victims of such accidents are not only motorists but also innocent pedestrians. The latter's right to cross the road when the green light is on is often violated by motorists, who are always in a hurry.

Pedestrians are not safe on sidewalks either. Motorcyclists, impatient to get ahead of vehicles in front of them, often invade sidewalks, leaving no space for pedestrians to use. There are also private cars and pick-up trucks permanently parked on sidewalks, in total disregard for municipal laws and civilized norms.

There is another problem – which the city can easily solve. The problem may not be as life-threatening as the ones discussed above. It affects mainly foreign tourists who rely on the city's public-transportation system. It is not the system's rickety buses that I am talking about. While all well-wishers of the city hope that the authorities recognize the danger such buses pose to public safety and take immediate remedial actions, they are aware that those buses cannot be ordered off the road overnight.

I am referring to the helplessness foreign tourists experience in figuring out the destination of the bus. As I mentioned earlier, most tourists in the city are backpackers. Backpackers, by definition, are low-budget travelers. They depend on public transportation to get around the city. The signboards on buses that indicate their destinations are of little help to them. Except for a few long-distance buses, the destinations are written in Kannada, the official language of Karnataka State. Those who don't know Kannada have to seek the help of half a dozen people to make sure that they are boarding the right bus. They would find it immensely helpful if the city can order right away that a line be added, in English, to what now exists only in Kannada, indicating the destination of the bus.

This suggestion doesn't come out of any disrespect for Kannada. There is no denying that the primary purpose of public transportation is to serve the public and that all pertinent information should be provided in a language that most people understand. The suggestion is made with a view to seeing Bangalore, which has already earned a place on the tourist map of the world, live up to its reputation.

English, to state the obvious, is the lingua franca of the world. Most cities around the world, interested in attracting foreign tourists, have already adopted the practice of providing travel-related information in English, in addition to the local language. Mumbai goes a step further in showing indifference to this need. And this, despite the city being the commercial capital of India. There, even the numeral indicating the bus route is written in Marathi, which in turn is derived from Devanagari. (Unless, of course, the traveler has enough time to run to the side of the bus before boarding it. On the side, thankfully, the route number is written in Arabic, as is the practice all over the world, and the destination in English.)

Beijing and Shanghai Are Far Ahead

Take the case of China, where English is not as widely used as in India. In Beijing and Shanghai, the two major cities of China, one can go places without knowing even a word of Mandarin. Buses and trains make announcements (pre-recorded) of approaching stops and stations in Mandarin as well as English. The public is very helpful, too. The educated among the Chinese rarely miss an opportunity to brush up their English when an English-speaking foreigner approaches them with a question. No wonder foreign travelers and business investors are flocking to China in droves, making it the fastest-growing economy in the world.

On the information technology superhighway, Bangalore may be far ahead of Beijing and Shanghai. But in making it tourist-friendly, it has a long way to go before catching up with the two Chinese cities. And this, in spite of the fact that Indians are far more facile with English, the language predominantly used in information technology, than the Chinese. Bangalore has yet to live up to its reputation as the Silicon Valley of India.

15

What Makes Islamic Turkey Different from Islamist Saudi Arabia**

I spent the last two weeks of November 2007, traveling around Turkey. I was part of a tour group from the United States. Apart from affording me an opportunity to learn a lot more about Turkey, the tour helped me reaffirm that a country can be Islamic without being Islamist and that Islam and democracy can coexist in any country, if the leaders and the led in that country have the will to accomplish it.

Calling Turkey Islamic may sound as odd as calling India Hindu, for this simple reason: Both countries are firm in their commitment to secularism and that commitment has been enshrined in their constitutions. I am calling Turkey Islamic partly because its population is overwhelmingly Muslim, most of them religious; and mainly to highlight how different it is from an Islamist country like Saudi Arabia.

Turkey is 98 percent Muslim. It is also 100 percent democratic. Its adherence to the two basic tenets of democracy – the separation of church and state; and equality before the law and equal protection of all by the law – is as steadfast as in any democracy in the world. Ever since Mustafa Kemal Ataturk, the founder of the Republic

---

** *This was based on my observation in 2007. Since then, Islamic fundamentalism has been making steady inroads on Turkish politics, undermining the country's democratic and secular tradition. A fear has been steadily mounting now that the country, which was indistinguishable from any West European country when I visited it in 2007, may soon end up looking like Saudi Arabia.*

of Turkey and its first president, decided to put the country on a democratic and secular path, in 1923, it has been distancing itself even from symbols and symbolisms one associates with Islam. Its ban on women wearing scarves in government offices and state-run institutions is a case in point

During the two weeks I spent in Turkey, I could count on my fingertips the number of women I saw wearing hijab or abaya. And the burqa, that stifling head-to-toe shroud the Taliban-type Islamist extremists force their women to wear? Not one. It only shows that, left to themselves, Muslim women would wear what they feel comfortable in. Most of the women that I saw wore Western-style dresses. That was the case with men, too. And men wearing the type of beard that has been touted by Islamist fundamentalists as a religious requirement were a rarity. When I mentioned to a Turkish friend in Istanbul that one could see more hijabs and abayas in India, where only 14 percent of the population is Muslim, this is what he said (I am paraphrasing it):

The Five Pillars of Islam

The Five Pillars of Islam – Shahadah (belief in the oneness of God and in Muhammad as His Prophet); Salah (praying five times a day); Zakah (alms-giving to the needy); Sawm (fasting during the month of Ramadan); and Hajj (pilgrimage to Mecca) – adherence to which makes a person a true Muslim, say nothing about dresses and beards. Even of those five, absolute adherence is demanded only to the first one. The other four are flexible, with individual circumstances allowing considerable latitude. Rules and regulations on dress and physical appearance, and the systematic relegation of women to an inferior status, have their origins in the interpretation of the Koran, over centuries, by mullahs. The more fanatical, self-righteous and self-serving the interpreter, the more stringent the rules and regulations.

With a smile on his face, my friend concluded: "We Turks are good Muslims. Most of us, at least. But we keep our faith strictly between us and Allah. We don't force it down people's throats as they do in Saudi Arabia and many other Arab countries." Pointing to the famous Sultanahmet Mosque, he added, "Go inside on any Friday. You will see the place packed with religious Turks."

An otherwise unremarkable experience I had during my two-week tour of Turkey drove home to me the difference between the lifestyle of women in Turkey and of those in Saudi Arabia.

Lifestyle of Turkish Women

It was 7 a.m., November 27. We had arrived in Istanbul, the largest and most cosmopolitan city in Turkey, the previous evening. The conducted tour of the city was to begin at 9 a.m. I decided to spend the two hours I had at my disposal exploring the neighborhood on my own. There was another reason for me to get out of the hotel that early: I was anxious to make a phone call to my niece living in Pune, India, who had got married the day before. And I wanted to do it using a pre-paid phone card and a public telephone. Using the phone in my hotel room would cost me a lot more. I had tried to call my niece the previous day, just before the wedding ceremony, but the call did not go through.

With the phone card in hand, I started walking, looking for a pay phone. The receptionist at the hotel had told me that there was one "around the corner." Maybe I missed the "corner" he was referring to. I kept walking. But for the few sanitation workers and early office-goers, the street was empty. What a contrast! The same street had been packed with shoppers and window-shoppers the previous evening. Looking at the good-looking men and women, most of them in fashionable clothes, I had said to my friends in the tour group, "This could as well be a busy street in any European city. Can you tell the difference?" To which Betty Lou, from Waite Park, Minnesota, had responded, "That's exactly what I have been thinking, too."

Though anxious to make the phone call, I was thoroughly enjoying the walk. After five minutes or so, I saw a woman, maybe in her 20s, who was walking in the same direction. She was wearing an overcoat (the weather was around 40 degrees, Fahrenheit). Because it was unbuttoned, I could see that she had a skirt and a jacket on underneath.

When I approached her, she greeted me with a broad smile and said, "Gunaydin [Good Morning]." I returned the greeting in kind, which made her smile broader. (I had, by then, learned from our tour guide how to say a few words – like "hello," "good morning," "good evening," and "good night" – in Turkish.) She took off her ear-piece – she was listening to music from an iPod – and said something in Turkish, which I took to mean, "What can I do for you?"

The response I gave, in English, might not have made any sense to her. But with the phone card I had in one hand and the signs I made with both hands, there was no mistaking of what I was looking for. She gestured to me to accompany her.

We walked side by side, close to each other, like two friends. During the 10 minutes we were together, I tried to have a conversation with her. I would say something in English, and she would respond in Turkish. I cursed myself for not having learned a few more Turkish words before I started the tour. Though she spoke only a few words of English, she was able to convey to me what she did for a living and at what time she had to be at work. She said "office secretary" and "eight o'clock" in English.

When we reached a small building, with a row of pay phones in front, I told her, "Thank you."

No, she was not ready to leave me as yet. She took the phone card from me, contacted the operator at the telephone exchange and said something, with the word "international" in it. Then she took from me the phone number in India I wanted to call and pressed all the numbers herself. I realized why my call the previous day did not go through. Once she got through to India, she handed me the phone, shook hands with me and said "good-bye."

The words that came out of my mouth did not adequately express the depth of my gratitude for her. For two reasons: my niece had already started speaking at the other end of the phone; and I was too overwhelmed by this total stranger's endearing nature and enthusiasm to help.

The first thought that came to mind during my walk back to the hotel was: "What punishment would she have received from the authorities, if we were in Saudi Arabia and she was seen walking with an 'infidel' like me?"

There was a reason why I thought about Saudi Arabia in particular. The sickening way the Saudi legal system treated a 19-year-old rape victim had been very much in the news at that time. She was gang-raped by seven men. As though the pain, indignity, humiliation, and condemnation by Islamist extremists, which the woman suffered as a result of being gangraped, were not enough, the highest legal entity in Saudi Arabia sentenced her to 200 lashes and six months in prison. What was her crime? She was seen alone with a man who was not related to her.

The Saudi justice ministry issued a statement, on November 24, justifying the sentence. The statement, as reported by Reuters, said: "We reiterate that judicial rulings in this virtuous country ... are based on God's book (the Koran) and the traditions of His Prophet (Mohammad) and that no ruling is issued without being based on evidence..."

Whoever said that only the Saudi interpretation of the Koran and of the traditions of the Prophet is correct? Even going by the literal meaning of what is said in the Koran, only "[t]he woman and the man guilty of adultery or fornication" are to be punished, and that too only "with 100 stripes." The clerics on the Supreme Judicial Council, which is the highest legal entity in Saudi Arabia, decided to outsmart the Prophet by increasing the punishment to 200 stripes and six months in prison. What are we to conclude from this? That a man and a woman can be together only to commit adultery or engage in fornication? That women are men's property? That they are incapable of taking care of themselves?

Civilized people around the world were outraged by the news. The fact that the Saudi king, in the wake of the outrage, pardoned the rape victim does not make the Saudi legal system less disgusting. The victim would be living with the stigma of this Saudi-manufactured scandal for the rest of her life. She has already gone into hiding, according to press reports, fearing punishment from her own relatives. The punishment would be death. They call it "honor killing" and they find justification for that also in their twisted interpretation of the Koran.

Abominable Saudi Practices

I can think of three reasons why the Saudi ruling clique is able to get away with their abominable practices: One, it can afford to ignore world criticism as long as Saudi Arabia is the world's largest producer of oil and as long as alternative sources of energy to replace it haven't been found; two, being the custodian of Islam's two holiest places, its interpretation of the Koran gets accepted as authentic by the gullible among Muslim believers; and three, the leader of the free world, the U.S., which never tires of preaching the importance of democracy and human rights to the rest of the world, has always been buddy-buddy with Saudi Arabia, despite its being one of the most authoritarian and undemocratic countries in the world. The buddy-buddy relationship will continue as long as big business in America needs Saudi oil to survive.

No wonder the Bush administration reacted to the Saudi verdict in the rape case (before the woman was pardoned) the way it did. "This is a part of a judicial procedure overseas in the court of a sovereign country," State Department spokesman Sean McCormack said, on November 19, 2007. "That said, most would find this relatively astonishing that something like this happens." Mark it: The U.S. State Department found the verdict only "relatively astonishing."

President Bush outdid the State Department when he said at his press conference, on December 4: "My first thoughts were these. What happens if this happened to my daughter? How would I react? And I would have been – I would have been – I'd had – I would have been very emotional, of course. I'd have been angry at those who committed the crime. And I would be angry at the state that didn't support the victim."

Bah! What a profound observation! Rape victims around the world are going to find the U.S. president's words very soothing.

Here is what well-wishers, like me, of Saudi Arabia have to say to the progressive-minded among the Saudis: Don't expect the leader of the free world to start a campaign to bring democracy to your country. The leader has learned from the killing fields of Iraq what high school children learn in their classrooms – that democracy cannot be imposed on a society from outside; it has to be built from within. The first step toward building it, in your case, is keeping the clerics in check; telling them to stop playing God. After all, Arabic is your mother tongue. Which means that you have access to the original version of the Koran. You don't need the interpretation of a medieval-minded mullah to understand it.

The model for your country should be Turkey, as it was before the latter-day encroachment of Islamic fundamentalism on it. You should do for your country what the Young Turks did for theirs in the 1920s. Who knows, one of you may emerge as the Kemal Ataturk of Saudi Arabia.

16

Monuments in Mexico City that Pose Challenge to the U.S.

As soon as I checked into the hotel in Mexico City, I pulled aside the window curtains and looked for what the hotel's website had featured as its special attraction: It "is located in front of the *Angel de la Independencia*," one of the most important monuments in the city. All I could see in front was a multistory building, with a garage at the level of the room I was going to occupy. I asked the bellhop who had brought my bags into the room whether that was the famous monument the vicinity of which the hotel touted as a selling point.

"That building came up a couple of years ago," he said. "It blocked the lovely view of *El Angel* we used to have from here." Mexicans usually use the short form, *El Angel*, while referring to the monument.

"Tell the hotel management to change the wording on the website," I told the young man. "It should say that the hotel is located in front of a monumental garage, not *Monumento a la Independencia*." He was embarrassed.

"It's not your fault," I said, placing a 20-peso tip (the equivalent of two U.S. dollars) in his hand. "You speak much better English than those guys at the front desk."

He smiled and thanked me "for those kind words." I felt happy that I helped him get over the embarrassment.

He did speak good English. In fact, he spoke better English than even the immigration and customs personnel at the Benito

Juarez International Airport, with whom I had to struggle to get my points across. I didn't understand anything the customs officer said, except "prohibited." He uttered the word while confiscating the 'contrabands' he found in my carry-on bag. The contrabands were an apple and a pear. I had forgotten to eat them before boarding the plane at the JFK International Airport, New York. This time, to Delta Air Lines' credit, the plane had taken off on time.

On many previous occasions, apples and pears had come to my rescue during my long, hungry waits at airports. Lately, long delays in departure and arrival of planes have become routine at most U.S. airports.

Angel de la Independencia

The next day, the first thing I did after getting up in the morning was to go looking for *El Angel*. It was built at the turn of the 20th century to commemorate the centennial of Mexico's war of independence. The war began on September 16, 1810, and ended on August 24, 1821. The Treaty of Cordoba that ended the war also ended three centuries of Spanish colonial rule in Mexico.

The Angel, which gives the monument its name, is represented by a 23-foot-tall statue of a woman with wings, symbolizing what Mexicans call the "Winged Victory" in their war of independence. The Angel holds a crown in her right hand and a broken chain in the other. The crown symbolizes victory and the broken chain freedom. The gold-plated bronze statue is perched on top of a 121-foot-tall column made of steel.

On four vertices of the quadrangular base of the column are bronze statues of four women, representing Law, Justice, War and Peace. In 1925, the remains of the heroes of the war of independence were interred in the basement. Since then, the basement has been revered as a mausoleum for those heroes. The monument, built on the beautiful Reforma Avenue (*Paseo de la Reforma*), is quite an impressive structure and a great tourist attraction.

The first time I saw *El Angel* was on the morning of April 9, 2008. The gold-plated statue shone brighter in the morning sun. My immediate reaction was to forgive my travel agent's failure to tell me that the hotel he had booked for me was not air-conditioned. The joy *El Angel* gave me more than made up for the tossing and turning I did all night in the stuffy hotel room. "But for the fact that the hotel is only two minutes' walk from here, I wouldn't have had this joy," I said to myself, taking in the beauty of the monument. I treated myself to that joy every morning, and a few evenings, of my one-week stay in Mexico City.

One evening, I was training my camera way up, on the face of the Angel, when I got distracted by a female voice. "Don't fail to take note of where the Angel is facing," the voice said.

When I turned around, I saw a middle-aged woman, in blue jeans and T-shirt, smiling at me. I guessed, from her blond hair and blue eyes, that she was of Spanish, not Mexican-Indian, descent. (My guess was right, she told me later. Her grandparents had immigrated to Mexico from Madrid.)

I smiled back and asked, "Where is the Angel facing?"

"Can't you see? She is facing north."

"What about it?"

"Do you know what is to the north of Mexico?"

"The Rio de Grande."

"Beyond that river, I mean."

That made me pause for a while. "Are you telling me that you have some problem with the United States?" I asked her.

"I have no problem. But no Mexican can forget what the Americans did to us. They grabbed half of Mexico. And now they want to build a wall to prevent a few poor Mexicans from entering their country, looking for menial jobs which most Americans won't do anyway. They should have built the wall before they grabbed our land."

I wished for a moment that the anti-immigration activists in the U.S. had been with me, listening to what the lady was saying. She was referring to the demand being made by some of them to erect a wall along the U.S.-Mexican border as a way of preventing Mexicans' illegal entry into the U.S. She was also referring to the defeat and loss of territory her country had suffered in the Mexican-American War of 1846-48. Many Mexicans even now call it the war of North American invasion.

In terms of the Treaty of Guadalupe Hidalgo that ended the war, Mexico was forced to renounce permanently its claim to Texas; and obligated to cede to the U.S., in exchange for mere 15 million dollars, what are now parts of present-day Colorado, Arizona and New Mexico, and all of California, Nevada and Utah. The remaining parts of Arizona and New Mexico States were acquired by the U.S. in 1853, in a deal that came to be called the Gadsden Purchase. The purchase price, which Mexican President Santa Anna was forced to accept, was 10 million dollars.

"Come with me," the lady, whose casual remark opened my mind to Mexico's history, said. "Let me show you another statue that reflects Mexicans' attitude toward the United States."

Diana the Huntress

We walked a few blocks on Reforma Avenue. When we reached the point where Reforma meets Sevilla Street, she stopped. Pointing to the statue of a naked woman posing as an archer, in the middle of a floral-shaped fountain at the intersection of the two roads, she said, "This is the Fountain of Diana the Huntress, another important landmark in the city. Though the statue is now called *la Diana Cazadora* or Diana the Huntress, the original name given to it by its sculptor was *la Flechadora del Norte* or the Northern Arrow Thrower."

The sculptor, Juan Olaguibel, had meant his work to be a monument, not merely to Diana, the Roman Goddess of Hunting, but to the beauty of female body as well. That's why he presented Diana in the nude. His model, it is said, was a 16-year-old part-time secretary who worked for Mexico's state-owned petroleum company. Story goes that she posed naked for the sculptor every day of the six months – from April to September 1942 – that took for him to complete the statue. The young lady's only compensation was the joy "of seeing her body immortalized on one of the most beautiful avenues in the city."

Diana's Nudity Draws Protests

But soon after the statue's inauguration, on October 10, 1942, Diana's nudity drew protests from Mexico's prudes. The forms of protest included covering the nudity with underwear made of cotton. Cotton underwear on a bronze statue? Sculptor Olaguibel had a better idea. He replaced it with one made of bronze. But hoping to take it off sometime later, when the Mexican society was expected to become less prudish, he welded the underwear at three corners only tentatively.

In the midst of Mexico City's much-trumpeted preparations to host the 1968 Olympics, Olaguibel petitioned to the government for permission to remove the underwear. The petition had the backing of a large number of Mexican artists and social activists. The government granted the sculptor his wish and the public once again began to enjoy Diana's beauty in its pristine form.

"You didn't drag me here to give a lecture on the covering and uncovering of Diana's nudity, did you?" I asked the Mexican lady.

"You are right," she said. "I didn't. I want you to take a look at the direction in which the arrow is pointed."

"Oh, Oh," I responded. "Here we go again. And what's the evil the Goddess of Hunting is trying to eradicate with her arrow?"

"I don't know," she said. "But I want you to know that the arrow is pointing northward. Once again, what is lying to the north of Mexico?"

"You have made your point," I said. "Let's talk more about it over a coffee."

We walked into a nearby coffee shop. Soon after ordering coffee – she ordered "Espresso," which was the most expensive coffee listed on the menu and I ordered "Coffee Americano," the cheapest – she apologized for "rudely disrupting" my photographing of *El Engel*. She said she "didn't want to pass up the opportunity I got to reminisce with an Indian the wonderful time I had in New Delhi a few years ago."

She had visited New Delhi on her way back from East Timor, where she had gone as a volunteer to monitor the election held under the auspices of the United Nations, on August 30, 2001.

"Don't be apologetic," I told her. "The evening has been quite an educative experience for me."

It was. Not just in terms of what I learned about two important monuments in Mexico City. Thanks to the time I spent with her, I got an insight into the thinking of Mexicans on what was then a hot-button issue in the U.S.

The anti-immigration campaigners were being naïve in thinking that erecting a wall along the Mexican border would solve the country's illegal-immigration problem. Mexicans detested the idea, as did most fair-minded Americans.

17

A Bridge on Austrian Border, a Memory Lane to Hungarian Revolution

Austria, especially its capital Vienna, had been on top of my travel wish list for a long time. For some reason or other, the travel plan fell through at the last moment all that time. At long last, in the summer of 2008, the plan materialized.

It was memorable in many ways; most importantly, for the visit I paid to the famous bridge at Andau, on Austria's border with Hungary. An otherwise unremarkable wooden footbridge, a little over 60 feet long, it became part of history for the role it played during the Hungarian Revolution of 1956. Today, it serves as a memory lane to that revolution and, for that reason, has become a tourist attraction. More about the bridge, in a minute.

Ever since my friend Kulamarva Balakrishna*** left Bombay (now Mumbai) in the late 1970s and made Vienna his home, I had an added incentive to visit the place. And he had been persistently inviting me to do it. The invitation that came in 1999 was in the form of an ultimatum, and quite an unnerving one. "Come now," it said.

*** *To get slightly ahead of the discussion, Kulamarva Balakrishna, an Indian journalist and social activist, passed away on February 27, 2013, in Vienna, Austria. Vienna had been his home since he left India in 1975, in the wake of the emergency rule imposed on the country by the late Prime Minister Indira Gandhi. He was one of the few fiercely independent journalists who were shadowed by Mrs. Gandhi's secret police. He left the country when his arrest became imminent. He is survived by his Austrian wife Eva and their son Bharat.*

"This may be your last chance to see me alive." He was preparing to undergo a major surgery to remove his defective pancreas.

For reasons beyond my control, I was unable to make the trip, even after that ultimatum. I sent him a letter, telling him not to have any misgivings about the competence of Austria's medical professionals. He would surely survive the surgery, I said in the letter, and both he and I would be around many more years, paying visits to each other many times.

As I had expected, the surgery was a success. And thanks to Austria's excellent healthcare system, which is accessible to the rich and poor alike, and to his strict post-surgery regimen and discipline, Balakrishna has been able to live a life more productive than most people who have their pancreas intact. Every day, he posts two or three articles on his blog, *Humans Austria*. The articles are social and political commentaries, often provocative. The blog is dedicated to "promoting human oneness and unity."

My reunion with Bala – that's what Balakrishna's close friends call him – brought back memories of the days we spent in Bombay as journalists. He had already been an established journalist by the time I started my career as a cub reporter on *Current* (now defunct), a weekly newspaper popular among the movers and shakers of Bombay at the time. Bala's exposé of Bombay's underworld had made him a well-known reporter in the city.

During the six days I was in Vienna, he took me around all important and interesting places in the city – museums, galleries, theaters, gardens, and parks. Almost every historic building in Vienna is an architectural marvel, with statues of historical figures adorning them. Even the power plant in the city, designed by Friedensreich Hundertwasser, is a piece of art.

Bala was more concerned about making my sojourn in Vienna comfortable than about his physical condition. I had to frequently remind him that he was on medication and that he had been advised by his doctors not to exert much.

His Austrian wife Eva joined us whenever she could. She is a painter by profession and makes a living working for a city-subsidized art gallery. The same gallery was going to hold an exhibition of her paintings the following week. At the time I was in Vienna, she was busy preparing for it. At their home, which doubles as Eva's studio, I had a preview of what she was going to exhibit. Most of the pieces that I saw were reflective of the people, places and events she had come across during her travels around India after marrying Bala.

During our wandering around, an exhibition going on at an art gallery near the one where Eva works caught out attention. An artist by the name of Peter Richnovsky was showing the photos he had taken during his visits to various parts of northern India. The India theme of the exhibition drew us into the gallery.

Looking at one photo, captioned "Mumbai," I commented, "No, the caption should be Kolkata, not Mumbai." The photo was that of a man pulling a rickshaw, with another man seated in it. One may witness many sickening scenes in Mumbai. But human beings pulling rickshaws, with fellow human beings sitting in them, is not one of them. That abominable practice still prevails only in Kolkata, formerly Calcutta. It's a shame that the Communist Party-controlled government of West Bengal, of which Kolkata is the capital, hasn't outlawed this inhuman practice as yet. And the Communists still masquerade as champions of the oppressed.

Only when we were coming out of the gallery did I realize that my comment about the caption was too loud. The man sitting at the entrance to the gallery had overheard it. I had not known that he was the photographer whose works were on display until he introduced himself and said, to my slight embarrassment, "Yes, the caption should have been 'Kolkata,' not 'Mumbai.'" He didn't blush when he said it.

Anachronistic Communists

The anachronistic Communists were very much the topic of our conversation when Bala and I visited the famous bridge at Andau, the next day. The visit was made possible by the kind gesture of Bala's Austrian friend who lives close to the Austro-Hungarian border. He had invited us to lunch at his home. Before the lunch, he offered to drive us to the bridge.

It was a pleasant 45-minute drive through the Austrian countryside. The narrow wooden bridge linking Austria and Hungary, which takes its name from the Austrian border village Andau, became world-famous during the 1956 Hungarian Revolution. The bridge served as an escape route for Hungarians who fled their country when Soviet tanks rolled in to suppress the revolution. Those who participated in it were ruthlessly attacked by Soviet troops.

The revolution was started by students and intellectuals, with a demand for removal of the Stalinist form of government, which the Hungarian Communists had imposed on their country, with Soviet blessings, and for restoration of democracy. It was steadily gaining momentum when the Soviet Union decided to send in troops and tanks to crush it. The Soviets feared that Hungary was on the brink of breaking away from the Warsaw Pact. About 2,500 Hungarians died in the Soviet onslaught and 200,000 (about 2 percent of the total population) fled the country.

Those who fled toward west crossed the bridge at Andau and ended up on the Austrian side, to the warm welcome and hospitality of the villagers there. It is said that, in three months since the revolution began, on October 23, 1956, about 70,000 people had escaped to Austria, using the bridge. Their plight has been vividly portrayed by James Michener in his famous 1957 book, *The Bridge at Andau*.

Michener was on the Austrian side of the bridge when the exodus began. Most of those who fled the Soviet tyranny, whose woes Michener recorded in his book, were young, their average age being 23. Among them were students, professors, writers, engineers and other professionals. From one university alone, 500 students and 32 professors and their families had fled.

The original bridge was blown up by the invading Soviet army on November 21, 1956, at the height of the revolution. It was rebuilt later, mainly to memorialize the revolution. A lookout-like structure has also been built, on the Austrian side, for the same purpose. The inscription on the structure shows how indebted the revolutionaries were to Austria. It reads (as translated by our Austrian host):

"Dear Austria, you are the first to be on our side in the freedom struggle. For your touching help and hospitality, we thank you from the bottom of our hearts.

> *— In the name of the Hungarian people,*
> *the students of the University of Sopron."*

The translation of the inscription, from the Hungarian language, may be approximate. Our host who rendered it had no pretense of being a linguist. His mother tongue is German, and he makes a living working as a gardener for the city administration of Vienna. When he told me that he had only a smattering of the Hungarian and English, I couldn't help saying to myself, "That's more than most Americans with university degrees and diplomas can say about themselves."

The lunch he and his wife treated us to was sumptuous. The quality wine he served us was from the winery owned by a family friend of theirs.

On our way back from the bridge, he had given us a tour of the winery, Scheiblhofer, and the surrounding vineyard. It was a Sunday, and the owner was working in the vineyard. Pointing to him, our host said, "Now you know how he built his business from scratch and made it into what it is today." Today, it is a successful winery that has started exporting its products to other countries.

The anachronistic Communists may want to learn a lesson or two from the success story of this Austrian vintner and from the lifestyle of our host who is just a gardener in Vienna. Under the Communist scheme of things, a gardener is supposed to be a member of the oppressed proletariat.

18

An Austrian-Muslim Woman Determined to Remain Modern

I was on my way from Vienna to Brussels. It was part of my eight-country European tour, in the summer of 2008, made possible by the affordable Eurail Pass.

Learning from the experience of those who had gone on similar tours before me, I had decided to do the traveling at night as much as possible. Traveling at night has two advantages: one, you will have more daytime for yourself to explore the new place you are going to be in the next day; and two, for less than what you pay at a hotel, hostel or bed-and-breakfast place, you can get a berth on a sleeping car on any long-distance train. In other words, you are saving time and money by traveling at night. But be prepared for an occasional disturbance on the train and the loss of sleep resulting from it.

I was not expecting any disturbance when I boarded the train at Vienna and found, to my pleasant surprise, that I had the entire six-berth sleeping car for myself. I went to sleep right away, hoping to wake up only at Frankfurt. At Frankfurt, I was to change over to a Brussels-bound train.

But the luxury of sleeping alone in a space meant for six did not last long. It was interrupted by someone rattling away on her cellphone. Though I was slightly annoyed in the beginning, the interruption turned out to be something I should thank for. Not just because the person who caused it was an attractive young woman.

That was an additional factor, all right. But what made it pleasant and memorable was the subsequent conversation I had with her.

I was watching through the corner of one eye her talking, giggling and, at times, stamping the foot on the floor of the train. Though I didn't know a word of what she was saying, because it was in German, I knew she was all excited. She was fair, blond-haired and blue-eyed. She was wearing blue jeans and a T-shirt. The light color of the lipstick blended well with her complexion. She appeared to me as a full-blooded Austrian.

"Are you going to Frankfurt?" I asked her as soon as she got off the phone.

"No, I will be getting off at the next stop," she said. "I got into this car because I saw some vacant seats here. I don't have any reservation. I grab any seat I can find during my daily commute between work and home. I am an intruder here. I hope you don't mind."

"Why should I mind?" I said. "I paid only for one berth. Moreover, who in the world would mind a pretty girl like you sitting next to him?"

"Thank you," she said, and gave me a beautiful smile.

"Now I know you also speak good English," I said. "I heard you speak German on the phone. What do you speak at home, English or German? How different is the Austrian-German from the original German?"

"No, I speak Arabic at home," she replied. "My parents are from Syria. They immigrated to Austria when I was just one year old. That was twenty years ago. I am very much an Austrian now. An Austrian-Muslim, I mean."

"You mean you are religious?" I asked her.

"Yes, in the sense that I believe in Islam and follow the religious practices to the extent possible. To the extent possible, because working full-time as a hairdresser and attending business school in the evening make it impossible for me to do the *namaz* five times a day. So, on weekdays, I do it once or twice and ask Allah for forgiveness for the ones I missed. But on weekends, when I am at home, I do it all five times. My parents tell me that such exemptions are permitted in exceptional circumstances. 'Allah is always merciful. Ask for His forgiveness whenever you feel you have done something wrong,' my father keeps telling me. Both my parents are religious. They have read the Koran from cover to cover. They say that many things in the Koran were practicable only in the seventh-century Arabia. According to them, our religion needs reforming. We keep such opinions within the family circle and go about living our lives like other Austrians."

Two-Inch Midriff

"You are lucky you have such enlightened parents," I told her. "Let me get one more curiosity out of the way. I like the way you dress. But do your parents approve of it?" I didn't specify it, but I was referring to her exposed midriff. Her low-waist jeans exposed part of her buttocks, too.

"So far, they haven't said anything about my dress. My mother teases me once in a while, though. 'Darling,' she used to say, 'you are asking for trouble.' My parents know that the profession I have chosen requires me to be modern, not only in mind but in appearance too." Then she posed this question: "How many Austrian women would go to a hairdresser who appears in a head-to-toe shroud?"

"You are expressing the kind of sarcasm I feel for the Taliban- and Wahhabi-imposed Islamic dress code," I told her.

She laughed. Then she opened up another personal side of her life: "In fact, I left my first boyfriend because he kept insisting that I give up jeans and T-shirt and dress in traditional Islamic ways."

"Is he that bearded variety?" I asked her.

"No, he is clean-shaven, always in jeans and T-shirt himself. Moreover, he drinks heavily, rarely prays and rarely goes to mosque, even on Fridays. And he wants me to move around like a black tent. I pointed out his hypocrisy during our last meeting that led to the breakup. 'Shame on you,' I told him before I walked away." She started getting a little agitated.

"Is he a Syrian, too?" I asked her.

"No, he is a Turk. Unlike me, he was born and brought up here. His parents came from Turkey years before he was born. When we met, he was not like this. He was as cosmopolitan as any Austrian boy in our class. His transformation began lately. I think the turning point was the American invasion of Iraq. He is a disgrace not only to Austria but even to Turkey. In fact, I told him so a few times."

I could relate to that. Most Turks that I know are progressive-minded Muslims. They keep their religious belief strictly between them and Allah.

"Your ex-boyfriend symbolizes a new trend: young Muslims enjoying the facilities and privileges provided by secular, modern societies, and then falling into the traps laid by fanatics like Osama bin Laden. Until this most-wanted criminal in the world is silenced, the trend will continue. By the way, who is your new boyfriend?"

"He is of Jordanian descent," she said, "a modern Muslim like me. An Austrian-Muslim, I mean. He is a gentleman. He treats me as an equal. He also has problems with many things in the Koran. Actually, the person I was speaking with was him. He is more fluent in German than Arabic. That's why you heard me speak with him in German. I am sorry I was so loud that I woke you up. My boyfriend is concerned that I am late. There is a 15-minute walk from the train station to my house. It's a pleasant walk. It's safe and I enjoy it. But he is concerned. He is coming to the station to fetch me. He is a gentleman."

"I am happy for you," I told her. "And I wish you all the best in the new relationship."

At that point, the announcement came about the next stop, where she had to get off. She thanked me for the "wonderful conversation" and shook hands with me. Accompanying her to the door, I said, "Would you mind telling your parents one thing for me?"

"What is it?" she asked.

"Because you spent the past 45 minutes with a guy who is not related to you, you are going to be punished by the mullahs with 100 lashes. The punishment is prescribed in the Koran."

"My parents have some choice words for those mullahs," she said, laughing. "But if what you say is true, it strengthens the arguments of my parents, me and all my close friends about the need for reforming our religion. But none of us have the guts to argue openly. I envy those who have."

I gave a peck on her cheek and said good-bye. Watching her exit the platform, I said to myself, "What a wonderful girl! If all Muslims were like her and her parents, Osama bin Laden would have to look for another planet to find followers. And Islam, in its reformed form, would find relevance to the modern world."

19

Manneken Pis and the Fuss Over Its Portrayal in Air India Ad

Manneken Pis, the famous statue in the Belgian capital of Brussels, had stirred a mini-controversy in India in the late 1960s. The reason? Air India had featured it in one of its advertisements. The advertisements were part of a campaign the airline launched to promote its recently introduced flights to various European cities, including Brussels.

Some prudes in Bombay (now Mumbai) did not like the idea of their national airline's using in its ads the picture of a child holding his penis and urinating. Air India explained to the prudes that the picture of Manneken Pis (meaning little man's piss, in the Dutch language), a statue that is a great tourist draw in Brussels, blended well with the theme of its ad campaign. The prudes wouldn't buy it. Nor were they mollified by the humorous twist Air India had given to Manneken Pis: The ad showed not only the little man pissing, but also a passerby warding off the 'urine' with an umbrella.

I was a journalism student in Bombay when the controversy erupted. I remember getting into heated arguments with some of those prudes who took Air India to task for the advertisement's alleged offense to Indian mores. They wouldn't even utter the word penis, let alone tolerate its portrayal in their national airline's advertisement.

I remember asking them: "What about the pictures that are hung on the walls of your homes and sculptures that exist in temples around India, showing gods and goddesses engaged in all kinds of natural acts, including sexual intercourse? And what about that adorable picture of Lord Krishna, as a child, eating stolen butter with one hand and fondling his penis with the other?" I even told them that, if I had money, I would drag them all to Brussels and force them to stand underneath the Manneken Pis statue and "take a picture of the piss falling on your heads." I knew even then that what came out of the statue was drinkable water.

Air India's advertisement and the controversy it generated came to mind during my visit to Brussels in the summer of 2008. After taking a good look at Manneken Pis and spending some time with the crowd around it, I requested a young lady from an Australian tour group to take a picture of me posing in front of it. "Make it look as though the piss is falling on my head," I told her.

I knew that there was no possibility of even that drinkable water falling on my head. The place where the statue stood and the water fell was fenced off. When some people in the crowd burst out laughing at my remark, I told them the story behind it. "There are such characters in every country," one of them said.

Legends Surrounding Manneken Pis

Legends surrounding Manneken Pis are many. One of them is linked to Duke Godfrey III of Leuven (or Lower Larraine). He was only two years old when he assumed dukedom, in 1142. The same year, a battle broke out between his troops and the troops of the Berthouts, the lords of Grimbergen. The battle took place in Ransbeke, the present-day Nederover-Heembeek. Hoping to get inspiration from the infant ruler, the troops of Leuven put him in a basket and hung it from a tree at the scene of the battle. The infant, they say, urinated on enemy troops and the latter lost the battle.

Another legend goes thus: In the 14th century, Brussels was besieged by French troops. They were about to destroy the city with explosives, which they had already placed at the walls of the city. When a little boy by the name of Juliaanske, who had been spying on the enemy, saw the fuse of the explosives burning, he urinated on it. It is said that the statue of Manneken Pis was built in honor of the little boy's urination that extinguished the enemy's burning fuse and saved the city from destruction.

A third legend has it that the statue was built by a wealthy merchant as a token of gratitude to the people of Brussels. He was on a visit to the city with his family. He had been wandering around, oblivious of the surroundings, when he suddenly found that his little son was missing. He and the other members of the panic-stricken family searched for the boy all over the city. Many city residents also joined in the search. The search ended, to the great relief of the family and amusement of others in the search party, when one of the latter spotted the little boy "happily urinating in a small garden." The Manneken Pis, according to this story, is a monument built by the merchant as a gift of gratitude to the Belgians who helped him find his darling son.

The Original Statue Was Stolen

The original stone statue, erected as early as 1388, was stolen and replaced several times. The two-foot-tall bronze statue, which we see today at the corner of the streets, *rue de l'Etuve* and *rue Chênet*, was created in 1619 by sculptor Jerome Duquesnoy.

Every time I passed by the statue – I did it three times – during my four-day stay in Brussels, there was a crowd of tourists jostling with one another to take a good look at it. "If only those prudes in Bombay who argued with me years ago had witnessed this scene," I said to myself, looking at the crowd that was admiringly and amusedly watching the Manneken (the little man) pissing, with the penis held between his fingers.

I was not lucky enough to see the little man in any of his 600 costumes. The costumes, "most of which are freaking hilarious," are on display at the Musée de la Ville de Bruxelles.

No matter what the prudes and puritans say, Manneken Pis will survive and continue to attract crowds from around the world.

There is no doubt about it. I wish I could say the same about the country in which the statue stands. The intense hostility that has been going on for a long time between Flanders in the northern part of the country and Wallonia in the south has raised real concerns about the survival of Belgium as one nation. It is my hope and prayer that Belgians would find a way to end the hostility and keep their beautiful country intact.

20

Norway, Though Expensive, Is Humane and Generous

A frugal traveler, left to his choice, tends to exclude expensive places from his itinerary. I nearly excluded Norway from mine during my European travel in the summer of 2008. Looking back, how happy I am that I didn't! Yes, Norway is expensive. But it's also one of the most beautiful countries I have so far visited. Its people are warm, friendly and generous. Those qualities help a visitor forget, minutes after arriving in Norway, the pinch of its being expensive.

Those qualities also find reflection in the policy the Norwegian government has adopted toward the less fortunate in the world. Thanks to that policy, Norway has become one of the most coveted destinations for those escaping war, persecution and poverty in their home countries. At the time I was in Norway, there were 14,431 asylum-seekers knocking on its doors. The largest group, 3,137-strong, was from Iraq. Most of them were the victims of the U.S.-led war in Iraq that began in 2003. As of January 2004, there were 13,373 Iraqis living in Norway. They are the third-largest immigrant group in the country, after Pakistanis and Swedes.

I got a taste of how expensive Norway is from the very first purchase I made in the country – a small cup of coffee and a plain croissant. When the Filipino coffee vendor at the central train station in Oslo, the country's capital, charged me the equivalent in

Norwegian krone of eight U.S. dollars, I couldn't resist remarking: "I should have taken my friends' warning seriously."

"What warning are you talking about?" he asked.

"That Norway is the most expensive country in the world. In New York, what I bought from you would cost me just a little over two dollars."

"Yes," he replied, "we are expensive." After a moment's pause, he added, with a smile, "We are also rich. We don't mind spending."

His smile and sense of humor reassured me that he was happy being in Norway. The country has a humane immigration policy, of which he was one of the beneficiaries.

The first road I hit after coming out of the train station was Karl Johans Gate. It is a for-pedestrians-only street that stretches all the way up to the Royal Palace. The Royal Palace is a landmark building in the city. Norway, being a constitutional monarchy, still reveres its king and treats his residence with respect. Travel guides also recommend it as a must-see place.

The bright morning sun of August added to the beauty of the surrounding areas and made my walk more enjoyable. I would have enjoyed it more, but for the worry I had of finding an affordable place to stay. For the umpteenth time, I had made the mistake of arriving in a strange city without knowing where I was going to stay. "When will I learn?" I asked myself, again, for the umpteenth time.

Henrik Wergeland

I was walking in the direction of the Royal Palace when a statue in a small park on the left side caught my attention. I learned from the epigraph on the pedestal that it is the statue of Henrik Wergeland. I didn't know the rest of what is inscribed. It is in Norwegian. I asked a man, who was sitting on a nearby bench and watching me take a picture of the statue, whether he knew who Wergeland was.

"Of course," he said, "every Norwegian who is familiar with his country's history knows who he is."

I said I was sorry, and added, "The one name from Norway's history that I always remember is that of the infamous fellow who betrayed his country to the invading Nazis during the Second World War."

"You mean Quisling?"

"Yes. I learned about him even as a teenager, when I read Jawaharlal Nehru's famous book, *The Discovery of India*. In that book, Nehru had used the word "quisling" as a synonym for traitor. He was referring to the quislings the British had created in India to prop up their colonial administration. I wonder whether you are familiar with the name Nehru. He was one of the leaders of India's struggle for independence from Britain. He was also the first prime minister of independent India."

"Of course, I am familiar with Nehru, Gandhi and many other famous Indian names. I am a great admirer of Gandhi. Wergeland belonged in the category of Nehru, Gandhi and such other noble souls. You shouldn't utter Wergeland and Quisling in the same breath. Henrik Wergeland was the exact opposite of Vidkun Quisling. He was not only a writer and a poet, but also a patriot of the stature of Nehru and Gandhi. Every Norwegian is proud of him. During his short life that lasted only 37 years [from 1808 to 1845], he accomplished a lot. Even now the Jewish community of Oslo visits his grave every year and pays homage to his memory. They do it in appreciation of what he had done to facilitate Jews' immigration to Norway. If he were alive today, he would be a vehement critic of the present government's policy. He was a defender of minority rights."

"But as far as I know," I said, "Norway's policy toward minorities is laudable."

"Maybe compared with many other countries," he said. "But we must do more."

"The rest of the world admires Norway for its religious and cultural tolerance," I told him.

He just smiled. "Enjoy your stay in the country," he said.

When I told him that I was looking for an inexpensive place to stay, he gave me direction to a couple of hotels.

I continued my walk, mulling over the contrast between the first two pieces of conversation I had after arriving in Norway: one, with a Filipino immigrant who was all praise for the country; and the other with a native-born Norwegian who, while proud of being Norwegian, was critical of its present government. Maybe the criticism came from his being very secure.

The impression I got from my conversation with him was that he was not one of Norway's Lutheran majority. About 86 percent of the country's population is Lutheran. And he didn't look like a member of its rapidly growing Muslim population. Almost all of them are of Pakistani, Middle Eastern and African origins. Thanks to the steady influx of immigrants from those regions, Islam has become the fastest-growing religion in Norway. Two percent of its present population is Muslim. He could be one of the 4.5 percent non-Lutheran Christians in the country or of its small Jewish minority. My strong guess was that he was Jewish.

After a few minutes' walk, I came across the first hotel he had given me the direction to. The "Room Available" sign at its entrance made me feel good. The good feeling, however, did not last long. The room turned out to be yet another reminder of Norway being very expensive.

When the woman at the hotel's reception desk collected from me the equivalent of 160 U.S. dollars, I was not expecting an attic. But that's what I got, an attic, with barely enough space to stretch my arms sideways. Other than the main door, the only opening the room had was on the roof. The only way I could let in some fresh air was by pushing its shutter up. Fortunately, it was not raining. So I pushed it – partly to let in some fresh air and partly to avoid feeling claustrophobic.

When I went back to the reception desk and complained that 160 dollars a night for such a room was a rip-off, the receptionist said, "You asked for the cheapest room, and I gave you one." She paused for a few seconds and continued, "About the price, hum, I know the feeling. We too complain about how costly things are around here."

"Why? Aren't you getting paid adequately?"

"Yes and no," she said. "The country is very good to us. But for any immigrant in any country, the beginning is always rough."

"Oh, you are not a Norwegian?"

"No, I am Polish. I came here two years ago. Again, the country has been good to me. I shouldn't be complaining. Once I get through these initial difficulties, everything will be OK."

She also told me that because there was a big conference, held by the International Geological Congress, going on in the city, all rooms had been booked several days earlier. "I wouldn't have given you that room, if a better one was available. Please go and have some breakfast. It is included in the rent," she said, pointing toward the adjoining room.

"I take back my complaint," I told her. "You are so sweet. There is something in the Norwegian air that makes people here very pleasant."

Another proof of that pleasantness came a few hours later. After the breakfast, a quick shower and a short nap, I went back to the train station, this time to buy a ticket for Bergen. Most travel books describe Bergen, the second-largest city in Norway, as more beautiful than the largest, which is Oslo. I had set aside my last day, the third day, in the country for a visit to Bergen.

After finishing my work at the ticket counter, I went to the locker room area of the station. Like most big train stations in Europe, Oslo's Sentralstasjon (central station) provides locker facilities, which passengers can rent for a day or two to keep their luggage. I had decided to keep most of my luggage in one of the lockers at the station, instead of schlepping it all the way to Bergen and back. Because I had some time to spare, I thought of getting familiarized with, right away, how the electronic lock worked.

A Happy Pakistani Immigrant

In the locker room, I was tinkering with the lock, when I heard a sweet female voice: "Can I help you?"

When I turned around, I saw an attractive, young, South Asian-looking, woman smiling at me. From the uniform – short skirt, shirt, and jacket with an epaulet on its shoulder – she was wearing, I could tell that she was an employee of the Norwegian State Railways.

After she finished showing me how the lock worked, I asked her, "Which part of South Asia are you from?"

"My parents came from Pakistan in the late seventies," she said. "I was only five when I arrived here. So I am very much a Norwegian now."

She could pass for a teenager. So I was surprised when she told me that she was a mother of two. She had a sister and three brothers. "All of us are very happy in this country," she said. The state-owned railways she was working for "treat the employees very well," she added. She worked as a train conductor and was thinking of switching to driving the train.

"Why do you want to switch?" I asked her.

"Because there is more money in it," she said.

"But there is also risk in it," I told her. "Just check the passengers' tickets and relax in a corner of the train when you have nothing to do. When you can afford to make life easy, why make it hard?"

She let out an endearing laugh.

"You made my day," I told her, shook hands with her and left the locker room.

Pakistanis were the first batch of South Asians to take advantage of the liberal immigration policy of Norway. The first batch arrived in the 1970s as "guest workers." Most of them were from the province of Punjab. There are close to 60,000 people of Pakistani origin living in Norway now. That's a considerable chunk in a country whose total population is less than five million.

The first batch of Pakistanis, as is the case with all new immigrants, had a rough time. But thanks to the generous help they received from the state, they were able to give good education and upbringing to their children. Almost all those children, now in their 20s and 30s, are doing very well. The young lady I met is a living proof of that.

"I should stop complaining about Norway being expensive," I said to myself while leaving the station. "As long as it is using part of its wealth to help the less fortunate in the world turn their lives around, I mustn't complain."

21

A Memorable Train Journey Across Mountainous Norway

Seventy percent of Norway is mountainous. A train journey across the country takes one around the valleys of some of them, through the tunnels dug into some others and to the peaks of still others. The awe-inspiring tunnels and panoramic views of the country one gets while on the train make the journey a memorable experience. I had that experience in the summer of 2008.

I was on my way from Oslo to Bergen. The capital city of Oslo, in the east, which is also the largest city in the country, sits at the mouth of a fjord. Bergen, the country's most beautiful and second-largest city, on the west coast, is the "gateway to the fjords of Norway." In the words of the well-known travel writer Rick Steves, "Norway's greatest claim to scenic fame is its deep and lush fjords." Looking out of the train window and taking in the stunning beauty of some of those fjords, I couldn't help cursing myself for not planning my trip thoughtfully so as to include a fjord cruise in it. I promised myself to do it, if and when I came to Norway again.

Adding to the joy of my seven-hour journey was the pleasant conversation I had with a retired Norwegian couple. The retired geologist and his wife, retired as a college-gym instructress, were going to Bergen to attend an open-air concert by their "favorite musician," Eric Clapton. The August 6 concert was part of Clapton's

"2008 Summer Tour," which began in the U.S., at Tampa Bay, Florida.

"Clapton used to be a favorite musician of mine, too," I told the couple. "In fact, I grew up as part of the rock 'n' roll generation in India. I was a great fan of Elvis Presley and, later, the Beatles."

"We, too," the husband said.

"Don't ask him to demonstrate the Elvis gyration," the wife added.

"We have something in common there also," I said. "I don't have, and never had, any illusion that I am a singer. But in my younger days, I used to sing all Elvis songs. And I never missed an opportunity to do his gyrations."

"Let's watch it," the wife said. "My husband will be happy to join you."

"I clearly said I used to do it in my younger days. If I do it now, I may slip my disc. I am sure you don't want me to end my Norway trip right here." Both of them laughed.

"Now," I continued, "to get back to Eric Clapton. I used to admire him a lot. He fell out of my favor when reports began to circulate, in the seventies, that he was a racist and a supporter of the anti-immigration policy of the controversial British politician, Enoch Powell."

"Rock Against Racism"

The "Rock Against Racism" campaign – which a few pop, rock and reggae musicians launched in Britain in the 1970s – was a direct response to Clapton's racist, anti-immigrant attitude and utterances in those days. The most disgusting of those utterances came during a concert in Birmingham, England, on August 5, 1976. It was reported that in the middle of the concert, after once again repeating Enoch Powell's favorite line – that Britain was in danger of becoming a "black colony" – he shouted: "Throw the wogs out. Keep Britain white." That was the pet slogan of the National Front, the racist organization that had poisoned British politics in those days.

"Of course, the report also said that Clapton appeared drunk throughout the concert," I told the couple. "But being drunk is no excuse for uttering such rubbish."

"We know he had problems with alcohol and drugs," the husband said. "He has turned his life around since then. But we always liked his music."

"There is no denying that," I said. "He was, and still is, a superb musician. How many musicians have been inducted into the U.S. Rock and Roll Hall of Fame three times?"

"Come and enjoy the concert this evening," the woman said. "Maybe you will once again start admiring him."

"I will certainly try. I have to catch the last train back to Oslo tonight. I couldn't get a room in any of the hotels in Bergen for the night. I didn't know that Clapton enjoys this much popularity in Norway."

The Longest Train Tunnel

While we were talking, the train had gone into and out of several tunnels. When it came out of one, nearly five minutes after going into it, I said, "This is the longest train tunnel I have ever gone through in my life. Is this the longest in Norway?"

"No," the man said. "Between Oslo and Bergen, there are 182 tunnels. But the longest one is not on this line. You pass through that tunnel on your way from Oslo to the airport." The 47,800-foot-long Romerike Tunnel (*Romeriskporten*, in Norwegian) was completed in 1999.

A few minutes later, the train stopped at a place called Finse. Finse is a skiing and hiking village. I could see snow on some of the surrounding mountains. Snow in August, the peak of summer? But then, it's Norway.

At 4,006 feet above the sea level, the Finse station is the highest train station in the entire Norwegian railroad system. A few more minutes later, the train stopped at a station called Myrdal, where many of the passengers got off. I asked one of them, "Are you from this place?"

"No, I am from Washington, D.C.," she said.

I gave her a surprised look. "A fellow living in New York had to cross the Atlantic to meet a woman living in Washington, D.C.!" I said. "And what are you doing here?"

"Don't you know?" she asked me, "this is where the Flam Railway [*Flamsbana*] begins. From here, I take a train to Flam. From Flam, I go on a sightseeing cruise through the famous Aurlandsfjord. After the cruise, I will be taking a bus back to this train line and resuming my journey to Bergen. I think I resume it at a place called Voss. The tour company that planned my trip strongly recommended this diversion on the way to Bergen. When I saw all these people getting off here to take the Flam train, I felt happy that I made the right decision."

"How stupid of me not to have done my homework. If only I had, I would have taken the diversion, too. Enjoy your trip," I told her and rushed back to the train, which was about to leave.

Back on the train, I told my new friends what I heard from the woman from Washington, D.C.

"Yes, that diversion is worth your time and money," the husband said.

"I read somewhere," added his wife, "that it is one of the world's most scenic rail trips." The couple had already enjoyed that, too. Then she went on to describe how scenic it was.

During the 12½-mile ride from Myrdal to Flam, the train descends 2,835 feet. It spirals its way through and around several mountains, making the descent smooth. It goes into and out of 20 tunnels. The numerous waterfalls, snow-clad mountains, and lakes, on the way, add to the thrill of the ride. "After the unforgettable ride," she said, "you reach Flam. Flam is unforgettable, too. It's a small place nestling in the midst of mountains."

"And the literal meaning of Flam is," the husband added, "the little place with steep mountains. Of course, in this part of the world, a place of five hundred people should not be called little."

Pointing to a few houses tucked away in a valley the train was passing by, he added, "That is considered a community here, with its own local administration. Some of them may have one or two policemen. And some have none. The need has arisen lately, though, for the presence of more policemen."

"I find policemen here very decent and polite in their dealings with people," I said.

An incident I had witnessed the previous evening, at a money-changing place in Oslo, was fresh on my mind. I was standing in a long line of people waiting to change their foreign currency into Norwegian krone. Suddenly, I saw a policeman come in and walk toward one of the cash-exchange counters. After a few minutes' talk with a lady sitting behind the glass-enclosed counter, he approached a man who was standing a few feet away from the line.

The man had a few days' growth of beard and was shabbily dressed. In physical features, he resembled some of the Ethiopians I had met during my wanderings around Oslo. It seemed he had been hanging around the money-changing place for quite some time, doing nothing, prompting the employees of the place to alert the police.

I heard the policeman say, "I don't want to know who you are. I don't want to know anything about you. And I don't want to know what you are doing in this country. But if you have nothing to do in this money-exchange place, please leave. By hanging around here doing nothing, you are making the employees of the place nervous."

The man paused for a few seconds and then left, without uttering a word.

After narrating the incident to the Norwegian couple, I added, "In most other countries, the first thing a law-enforcement official would say to a suspicious-looking person, especially a foreigner, is to show some ID. Here, not only did the policeman not ask for any ID, but he also thanked the foreigner when he left the scene politely."

"Did he look like a Romanian?" the husband asked me.

"No, he looked like an Ethiopian," I said.

"Romanians, some of whom are here illegally, have been causing a lot of trouble. Almost all beggars you see on the streets are from Romania. Begging is an organized crime the Romanians have been engaged in in this country. The beggars have bosses. Part of the proceeds from begging goes to the bosses. Here, people living in small towns, seldom lock their houses. Soon they will have to."

That is the price the Norwegians are made to pay because of the country's open-door policy toward those running away from war, persecution and starvation. Then he shared with me another concern caused by that policy.

State Supporting Osama bin Laden?

The Norwegian constitution, though democratic and secular, still permits some ties between church and state. One form of those ties is the financial support the state has been providing to the church. When the constitution was adopted in 1814, the population was almost entirely Lutheran and the only church the state had to support was the Lutheran Church. As the support went to the benefit of the people as a whole, there was no problem. But now, though Lutherans are still in an overwhelming majority (86 percent of the population), there are also other religious groups in the country. It has become necessary for the state to re-evaluate the policy of supporting the church.

Faced with the option of either stopping the support altogether or equitably extending it to all religious denominations, Norway chose the latter. The constitutional amendment, agreed upon in April 2008 by all legislative factions, provides for equitable financial support to all religious groups, and even to atheist communities, in the country. "The possibility of state funds going to institutions run by Osama bin Laden's supporters cannot be ruled out," my new Norwegian friend said. "It will be interesting to watch how the government resolves the dilemma when the amendment is passed."

"Islam is growing fast in Norway," he hastened to add. "As long as we have Muslims of the type that came from Pakistan, there won't be any problem. They are well integrated into our society. But the wars in Afghanistan and Iraq have sent many Al Qaeda-type extremists into the country. Some sneaked in illegally. And some came in the garb of refugees. People are really concerned."

By then, the train arrived in Bergen. "I am so disappointed that our conversation has to end when it just started getting very interesting," I told the couple.

"Do come to the concert, if you have time," the husband said. "I am sure you will like it."

"And if for any reason you are not going back to Oslo tonight," the wife added, "come and have a drink with us." She gave me the name and phone number of the hotel where they were going to stay.

"I will certainly do it," I said.

I gave them a hug and got off the train, exclaiming: "Wow!"

22

Dachau Concentration Camp Memorial: A Chilling Reminder of Nazi Atrocities

You may have read volumes and volumes about Nazi concentration camps. You may have seen pictures and pictures of the atrocities the Nazis committed in those camps. But setting foot in what was once an actual concentration camp is an entirely different experience. It evokes an eerie feeling in you. I had such a feeling when I visited the Nazi Concentration Camp Memorial at Dachau, Germany, on August 15, 2008.

The Nazis came to power in Germany on January 30, 1933. They anointed Adolf Hitler as Chancellor of their proud *reich*. *Reich* in the German language means empire. Germany under Nazi rule (1933-1945) was also known as the Third Reich.

"Taking care" of all political enemies was the first item the Third Reich had on its agenda. The first step toward carrying out that agenda was to imprison all those enemies. But those whom the Nazis branded as enemies were too numerous for the space available in the existing prisons in the country. And they were in no mood to wait until new prisons could be built to incarcerate the enemies. They decided to convert an abandoned munitions factory at Dachau, 10 miles from Munich, into a makeshift concentration camp. In due course, the old factory building was demolished, and a full-fledged,

32-barrack camp came up in its place. Prison labor came in handy for its construction.

Heinrich Himmler, the police chief of Munich, officially opened the camp on March 22, 1933. When, at the opening ceremony, he called it "the first concentration camp for political prisoners," he was indirectly declaring that many more such camps would soon follow.

And many more did, all modelled on the one at Dachau. The Dachau camp also served as a training facility for guards and officials who would run the subsequent camps. Adolf Eichmann, "the architect of the Holocaust," and Rudolf Hess, who rose to become Hitler's first deputy before he fell out of his favor, were among those trained at Dachau.

Though anti-Semitism had been an integral part of the Nazi ideology from the very beginning, singling out Jews for persecution had not yet become an official Nazi policy at the time the Dachau camp was opened. The enemy list at the time consisted mainly of Communists, Social Democrats, trade unionists, and others who opposed the Nazi ideology. If there were Jews in the first batch of internees at Dachau, it was not because they were Jews but because they belonged to one or other of the groups in the enemy list.

Pastor Martin Niemöller

In fact, the internee, whose memorable words are quoted even now to castigate those who refuse to see evil as long as it doesn't affect them, was not a Jew. He was a Lutheran pastor. The words of Pastor Martin Niemöller (as translated by Bob Berkovitz), which stirred the collective conscience of the world when they were first published, are:

> When the Nazis arrested the Communists, I said
> nothing; after all, I was not a Communist.
> When they locked up the Social Democrats,
> I said nothing; after all, I was not a Social Democrat.
> When they arrested the trade unionists,
> I said nothing; after all, I was not a trade unionist.

When they arrested the Jews,
I said nothing; after all, I was not a Jew.
When they arrested me, there was no longer anyone
who could protest.

Jewish prisoners began to arrive at Dachau in large numbers in the aftermath of *Kristallnacht* or "The Night of Broken Glass." The notorious incident occurred on the night of November 9, 1938, when news reached the Nazis of the assassination of Ernst vom Rath, a diplomat of the Third Reich working in Paris. The assassin was Herschel Grynszpan, a 17-year-old German-born Jew. His parents were Polish immigrants in Germany. The reason he gave for his action was the humiliation his father and other members of his family suffered at the hands of the Nazis back home.

On October 27, Grynszpan's family and over 15,000 other Jews, all of whom were originally from Poland, had been expelled from Germany without any warning. They were put in boxcars, taken by train to the Polish border, and dumped there.

"Final Solution of the Jewish Question"

Even before *Kristallnacht*, discrimination against Jews had become an official policy of the Third Reich. It attained legal status in 1935, with the enactment of what was called the Nuremberg Laws. The laws began to be enforced with a vengeance in the wake of the Nazi diplomat's assassination in Paris by a Jew. With that enforcement, discrimination against Jews began to take the form of state-sponsored persecution. Hitler and his propaganda minister Joseph Goebbels incited their fellow Nazis to "rise in bloody vengeance against the Jews."

Their vengeful acts led to the deaths of 91 Jews and arrests of over 25,000. More than 200 synagogues were destroyed, and thousands of Jewish homes and businesses were ransacked. Of those arrested, over 10,000 were brought to the Dachau camp. The finale of the state-sponsored persecution was the Holocaust, which was the answer that

Hitler's sick mind came up with after searching for a "Final Solution of the Jewish Question."

Dachau predated the "Final Solution" policy. That policy was pursued at concentration camps set up later, such as the one at Auschwitz. Of the 31,591 registered prisoners who died at Dachau (the actual number will never be known because the Nazis didn't bother to register thousands of those who were randomly caught and brought to Dachau), only about 5,000 were Jews. They all died because of the harsh conditions that prevailed in the camp. How harsh were those conditions? The daily routine they were forced to follow should give an idea.

From the wake-up call at 4 a.m. (which was mercifully moved to 5 a.m. in the wintertime), till the "Everyone in Bed" order at 9 p.m., all were kept busy doing something or other. Even the roll call was a form of rigorous punishment. A photo captioned "Prisoners at roll call," taken by Friedrich Franz Bauer and commissioned by the Nazis themselves, has this text underneath: "In the morning and the evening the prisoners had to line up in the roll call area to be counted. Irrespective of the weather, they were forced to stand at attention. The torture could drag out for hours."

The motto of the camp was "ARBEIT MACHT FREI [work makes one free]." Visitors to the memorial can see it displayed on the main gate.

True to the motto, the inmates were made to work all their waking hours. They were employed in the operation of the camp, on various construction projects, and in small handicraft industries established in the camp. They built roads, worked in gravel pits, and drained marshes. At the height of World War II, they were also used in armaments production. Those who were found unfit to work were summarily executed. The firing range and the gallows in the crematoria area still bear evidence to it. Some of the sick and weak prisoners were sent to the euthanasia center set up in the Hartheim castle, in the Austrian village of Alkoven, near Linz. Several thousand Dachau prisoners were killed at the Hartheim euthanasia center.

Prisoners Used as Guinea Pigs

Hundreds of prisoners also died or were permanently disabled as a result of experiments conducted on them by Nazi physicians. Prisoners were used as guinea pigs – in high-altitude experiments (using a decompression chamber), malaria and tuberculosis experiments, hypothermia experiments, and experiments to test new medications. Prisoners were also forced to test methods of making seawater potable and of halting excessive bleeding.

A note left behind by one of the prisoners still hangs on the wall of the cell in which he languished. Its English translation reads: "Four months in the Bunker, four months' detention in darkness, four months with hot food only every fourth day! Time crawls by. I only count every fourth day, and I'm amazed when the food comes and wakes me up – I'm in a state of trance."

The note was written by one Erwin Gostner, the prisoner in Cell No. 19, in July 1938. (That he at least remembered the month is remarkable.) After reading the note, I stood still for a while in front of the cell. "Was he left for dead by guards, when they came around at reveille to make sure that all prisoners were out of their cells, and in the roll-call area?" I wondered.

American liberators arrived at Dachau on April 29, 1945. As they came close to the camp, they found more than 30 railroad cars filled with bodies, all in an advanced state of decomposition. They later learned that those bodies were of prisoners whom the Nazis had hastily evacuated from camps in the front areas, before Americans could rescue them, and brought to Dachau.

When American troops entered the Dachau camp, they found over 30,000 inmates crowded into an area that was built for 5,000. Not long before the liberation, there were 67,000 registered prisoners at the Dachau camp. As news reached prison officials of the imminent arrival of Americans, they had pushed thousands of prisoners out of the camp and put on a "death march." Several thousand died in that march. Those who survived were rescued by Americans later.

In the words of the late Lt. Gen. William W. Quinn, who as a colonel in the Seventh U.S. Army had participated in the Dachau liberation, "Dachau, 1933-1945, will stand for all time as one of history's most gruesome symbols of inhumanity. There our troops found sights, sounds and stenches beyond belief, cruelties so enormous as to be incomprehensible to the normal mind. Dachau and death were synonymous."

23

Tamil Tigers Still Active in Europe. To Destroy India Is Their Next Goal

I had sat on this story for several months before publishing it. I first published it in The East-West Inquirer, an online monthly I edit, on February 21, 2010. The reason for my reluctance to publish the story soon after I hit upon it was my fear that, by doing it, I would be causing unnecessary alarm in India.

"But then," I asked myself, again and again, "what about the consequences of not publishing it? Don't I have a responsibility to alert India on the possibility of another terrorist attack? Will I be able to forgive myself if the self-proclaimed Tamil Tiger from Sri Lanka did mean what he said and carried out the threat he vowed he would? How can I forget the fact that the terrorist attacks of September 11, 2001, which changed the world for the worse forever, could have been prevented if only those in power in the U.S. at the time had not ignored the clear warnings they had that Osama bin Laden's Al Qaeda was determined to attack America? And what about the warnings India had about a possible terrorist attack in Pune, in the State of Maharashtra? The Pune attack – a terrorist-bomb explosion – took place on February 13, 2010. Wouldn't India have saved itself a lot of agony, if it had taken the warnings seriously and taken precautionary measures?"

Questions like these helped me get over my initial reluctance to publish the story. The essence of the story is that the Liberation

Tigers of Tamil Eelam (LTTE), which waged a guerrilla war in Sri Lanka for over a quarter century to carve out a separate homeland for the Tamil minority in that island nation and was defeated by the Sri Lankan army in May 2009, is still active in Europe. If the words of one of the Tigers are to be believed, its next target would be India.

On August 14, 2009, I was in Copenhagen, Denmark. It was the last evening of my 30-day tour of Europe, before leaving for New York the next morning. After wandering around the city until I couldn't drag my feet any longer, I ambled into an internet café.

I visit internet cafés while traveling around the world mainly to check my emails and browse the online editions of some of my favorite newspapers. This time, I accomplished more than that. My visit became instrumental in gathering some information that could be of vital interest to India and a few Indian officials.

As soon as I walked in, my eyes fell on an Indian-looking man sitting at one of the computer terminals. He took a good look at me. "You can use this terminal," he said, pointing to the one next to him.

"Thank you," I said. As I sat down, I realized that I made a mistake in accepting his offer: He badly smelled alcohol.

"Are you from India?" he asked me.

I said yes. "Are you?" I asked him.

"No," he said, in a tone that indicated that he was offended by my question. "I am a Tamil Tiger from Sri Lanka who has been living in Europe for the past 20 years."

In every Western European city I visited, I have come across many Tamils. Most of them are from Sri Lanka. Almost every South Indian-looking guy I ran into in Paris was a Sri Lankan Tamil. They all presented themselves as the victims of the civil war that had been going on in their country. Some of them could as well be Tamil Tigers clandestinely working among Sri Lankan émigrés to raise money and material support for their guerrilla campaign.

It's no secret that the LTTE, the guerrilla outfit Velupillai Prabhakaran put together in 1976, grew into a formidable force with its own army, navy and air force, because of the support it received from Sri Lankan Tamils living in Western Europe and

North America. But they all extended their support discreetly. This was the first time I met one who proudly and loudly proclaimed that he was a member of the LTTE. And he was proclaiming it while living in a country that has banned it. In all, 32 countries, including the U.S., the U.K., India, and Canada, have declared the LTTE as a terrorist organization. Among them, 27 are members of the European Union.

"I hate India," the shabbily-dressed Tiger said, and then asked, "Which part of India are you from?"

"I was born and brought up in Kerala," I told him.

Before I could tell him where I live now and when I left Kerala, he shot the next question: "Why do Malayalees hate Sri Lankan Tamils?"

"What do you mean?" I asked him. "I don't know any Malayalee who hates Sri Lankan Tamils simply because they are Sri Lankan Tamils. After all, both come from the same ethnic stock, and both have similar cultural background."

Three Malayalees on LTTE's Enemy List

My stress on our common bond made little impression on him. He spelled out the reason for his, and admittedly the LTTE's, hatred for Malayalees: The LTTE lost the war it fought against the Sri Lankan army because of three Malayalees – M. K. Narayanan, Shiv Shankar Menon, and Vijay Nambiar. Mr. Narayanan, who took over as governor of West Bengal on January 24, 2010, was a legendary figure in India's intelligence community for nearly half a century. It was what he did in his capacity as national security adviser, from 2005 until he became governor, that the Tamil Tigers detested.

Shiv Shankar Menon, who was recalled from retirement to take over from Mr. Narayanan as national security adviser, was one of the ablest foreign secretaries India had since its independence. During his tenure as foreign secretary, he allegedly did things that made the Tamil Tigers mad.

Mr. Nambiar has held many responsible and respected positions at the United Nations. Among them was the position he held as chief of staff under Secretary General Ban Ki-Moon, from January 2007 to December 2009. He has been special adviser to the Secretary General on Myanmar since 2010. However, it was his work as India's permanent representative at the U.N., from 2002 to 2004, that earned him the wrath of the LTTE.

According to the drunken Tiger, it was "because of the stupidity of those three Malayalees that the Sri Lankan government received intelligence on our [the Tamil Tigers'] movements and it was because of the naval blockade imposed by India that we stopped receiving weapons from abroad. And because of that, we lost the war."

What he said did not sound like the opinion of one individual. It sounded like something that was discussed at higher levels of the LTTE leadership. For that reason, I decided to sit and listen to him, suffering the stench of alcohol that came out of his mouth and the embarrassment I felt every time he bad-mouthed India and invited the attention of others sitting nearby. I was hoping to glean from his drunken outbursts anything that could be useful to India and to those whom the LTTE had put on its enemy list.

"Velupillai Prabhakaran may be dead," he continued. "But let India not be under any illusion that the war is over. It will not be over until we Tamils destroy India."

Velupillai Prabhakaran and the Tamil Question

Velupillai Prabhakaran, the founder-leader of the LTTE and one of the most feared terrorists in the world, died on May 18, 2009. He was gunned down by Sri Lankan troops while trying to flee the battle zone in an ambulance van. By the time the LTTE admitted defeat in what was one of the longest civil wars in Asia, it had claimed the lives of nearly 80,000 people, most of them innocent civilians. The victims were Sinhalese as well as Tamils. Many of the Tamils who joined his guerrilla outfit did so under duress. A large number of them were young girls and boys and some of them were kidnapped.

Those whom the LTTE sent on suicide missions were sent at gun point. In fact, suicide bombing, which is now so common among Islamist insurgents, was the brainchild of the LTTE.

True, Prabhakaran founded the LTTE, on May 5, 1976, with good intentions. He did it to redress the grievances of his Tamil brethren. The grievances were caused by a series of short-sighted measures adopted by the Sri Lankan government that were discriminatory to the Tamil minority. The Tamil minority in Sri Lanka constituted 30 percent of its population. Until those measures came into force, the Tamils were a contented, prosperous minority in the country.

The first discriminatory measure against the Tamils came in the form of the Official Language Act. Passed in 1956, it replaced English with Sinhala as the country's official language. Most Tamils, descendants of those brought in from India by the British to work as plantation laborers and clerks, were fluent in English. Their mother tongue being Tamil, and the official language of the country being English, they had not bothered to acquire even a working knowledge of Sinhala, the language of the Sinhalese majority. The new language act, which the Tamils dubbed "the Sinhala only act," forced large numbers of them to quit their jobs in civil service. The language requirement in recruitment tests made it virtually impossible for new ones to get in.

Then came the attempt by the Sri Lankan government to elevate Buddhism, the religion of the Sinhalese majority, to the status of state religion. Of the 30 percent Tamil minority, half were Hindus and the remaining half equally split between Muslims and Christians. Almost all of them were of Indian origin, and many still have their relatives in the Indian state of Tamil Nadu.

Naturally, India was concerned. It feared incurring the wrath of its vast Tamil population, if it remained unresponsive to Sri Lankan Tamils' grievances. It also feared a mass exodus of them to India. After all, the two countries are separated by a strait which is only 25 miles wide. All this meant that the Indian government could not afford to be indifferent to what was going on in Sri Lanka.

When Velupillai Prabhakaran moved to India, set up home and started LTTE training camps in Tamil Nadu, in September 1983, the Indian government under Prime Minister Indira Gandhi chose to look the other way. Though not wise as a foreign policy decision, India was left with no other choice. It could ill-afford to overlook the fact that most people of Tamil Nadu had expressed support for the cause the LTTE championed.

Whatever gains the LTTE made in the early stage were attributed to the help it received from the intelligence apparatus of the Indian government, the Research and Analysis Wing. But when the LTTE took to terrorism to advance its cause, the Indian government decided to distance itself from it. Other governments around the world, which until then had been sympathetic to the legitimate grievances of Sri Lankan Tamils, also became disgusted with the terrorist tactics Prabhakaran and his followers resorted to. India, which had already earned the displeasure of both the government and the Sinhalese majority in Sri Lanka – they even accused India of interfering in its internal affairs – now became a target of attack by the LTTE as well.

A disenchanted Prabhakaran quit India, in January 1987, and relocated his training facilities to Sri Lanka. The guerrilla war against the Sri Lankan government, which he had been directing from India since 1983, now intensified. Swathes of land in the Tamil-dominated areas in the north and east of the country came under LTTE control.

India Signs Peace Treaty with Sri Lanka

On June 5, 1987, when the Sri Lankan army laid siege to Jaffna, the largest city in the LTTE-controlled area, India ordered its Air Force to airdrop food parcels in the city. It feared that inaction on its part would lead to starvation and deaths among the innocent Tamils caught up in the war. The LTTE did not show even an iota of appreciation for what India did. The Sri Lankan government, as was expected, repeated its interference charge against India.

Then came another strategic move on India's part which the LTTE found outrageous. On being requested by the Sri Lankan government, India signed a peace accord with it. In terms of the accord, signed on July 29, 1987, between Prime Minister Rajiv Gandhi of India and President J. R. Jayawardene of Sri Lanka, India sent nearly 50,000 troops to Sri Lanka. The chief mission of the troops, known as the Indian Peace Keeping Force (IPKF), was to disarm the LTTE and enforce peace in the war-torn area.

Prabhakaran took the India-Sri Lank accord as a betrayal and vowed to "teach India a lesson." A prolonged armed struggle ensued between Indian soldiers and LTTE guerrillas. Indian forces suffered heavy losses. The presence of foreign troops on their soil did not go well with the majority Sinhalese population either. In 1990, a humiliated India withdrew its troops from Sri Lanka.

India might have made many mistakes in whatever it did during the protracted civil war in Sri Lanka. But there is no mistaking that it did it in the interests of the Tamil minority there and of millions of Tamils back home. I was surprised that the Tamil Tiger who was lecturing me was under the impression that his terrorist outfit still enjoyed the support of all Tamils living in India.

"Do you know there are sixty million Tamils living in India?" he asked me. "They are our brothers. They will join us in our war against India."

That, I knew, was wishful thinking. Not even all Tamils living in Sri Lanka were willing to join the LTTE. Most of them considered themselves victims as much of LTTE terrorism as of the means employed by the Sri Lankan army to crush it. Now that the war is over, they have the additional burden of proving to their government that they were victims, not supporters of the LTTE.

Hoping to hear the drunk blurt out something about any secret plan he and his fellow Tigers might be hatching against India, I patiently listened to him. "India thinks it is a big power," he continued. "Why is it that the big power doesn't have a single friend among its neighbors?"

The reason, which I didn't bother to tell him, is obvious: A big power, like a wealthy household, is always an object of envy among its neighbors. It is resented by them.

"Sri Lanka," he continued, "is befriending Pakistan and China, not India. Why is it so?"

The reason, again, is obvious: befriending your enemy's enemy is a sure way of strengthening your position vis-à-vis your enemy. This is not to say that the Sri Lankan government's attitude toward India has been inimical all the time.

The Tamil Tiger went on to say that the LTTE was determined to exploit all of India's troubles. He listed those troubles thus: "Kashmiri militants are fighting to break away from you. Maoist guerrillas are fighting against you in the north and northeastern areas. You have troubles on borders with Bangladesh. Pakistan keeps sending terrorist bombers into your country."

Hatred for Sonia and Rajiv Gandhi

The target of his ire then turned to Sonia Gandhi and her late husband Rajiv Gandhi. He justified with great relish the assassination of Rajiv Gandhi. The assassination, by a girl suicide bomber sent by the LTTE, took place on May 21, 1991, at an election rally in Tamil Nadu. According to this sadistic Tiger, it was "Rajiv Gandhi's reward for the harm he did to us." The "harm" he was referring to was the sending of Indian peacekeepers to Sri Lanka that is discussed above. Maybe the assassination was what Prabhakaran had in mind when he vowed to "teach India a lesson."

Every time the drunk uttered Sonia Gandhi's name, he prefaced it with the b-word. It was embarrassing for me to hear it. "She was a restaurant waitress," he said. "Rajiv Gandhi fell for her after a one-night stand. How stupid one could get."

I wanted to tell him that whatever political stability India has been enjoying since Rajiv Gandhi was killed was largely due to Sonia Gandhi's leadership of the Congress Party. But refrained from doing it for fear that my remark would only make him add the f-word to the b-word he had been spewing.

According to him, India is on the brink of breakup. I couldn't tell whether it was the outburst of a drunk or the thinking of Tamil

Tigers who he said were still active in Europe and America. If the latter is the case, it may be prudent for India not to laugh it away as the Bush administration did when ominous warnings came from Osama bin Laden that he was determined to attack America.

True, the LTTE has been reduced to a rump after the deaths of Velupillai Prabhakaran and his trusted lieutenants. But the capability of even a rump to wreak havoc should not be underestimated. An important lesson we learned from the 9/11 terrorist attacks on the U.S. is that it doesn't take a superpower to hurt and humiliate another superpower. A few misguided youngsters can do it, if fired with fanaticism and provided with the wherewithal.

24

What India and Virgin Mary Have in Common

COPENHAGEN, Denmark; August 15, 2009: August 15, to state the obvious, is the most important day on India's political calendar. Most politically conscious Indians wake up on this day with their country very much on their minds. That's the case with me, too, when I woke in my hotel room in this Danish capital, early this morning.

I thought about the marvelous progress India has made since it attained independence from British colonial rule 62 years ago today. I once again thought about what I consider the country's proudest achievement since independence: its steady development into a mature democratic polity, in spite of having been on the brink of disintegration many a time.

"How many countries in the world, which emerged from colonialism or other kinds of authoritarianism, about the same time as India did, can boast the kind of democratic continuity in governance as India can?" I repeated the question for the umpteenth time. This time, of course, to myself. This time, being a solitary wanderer in Europe, there was nobody around with whom I could share my thoughts. While most former colonies that became independent about the same time as India are still struggling to establish their national identities, India is well on its way to becoming a world power.

Today is the last day of my month-long learning-cum-pleasure tour of Europe. My flight to New York is scheduled to leave at 12:20 p.m. Which means that I have a few hours to spare before leaving for the airport. "What better way to spend those hours than to celebrate India's independence," I said to myself. "And what better place to do it than at the embassy of India in the city. I don't think there will be any Indian embassy anywhere in the world which doesn't have some celebratory event on this day. Also, I may get an opportunity to meet some fellow Indians living here." With a heart filled with thoughts like these, I left my hotel room and headed to the Indian embassy in Copenhagen.

The embassy is a bit far from the city proper. After a 20-minute train ride from the central train station, I got off at a place called Svenemollen, as instructed by Yashpal from New Delhi who owns a pizzeria in this city. There was hardly anyone on the street to seek direction from. It was 8 o'clock in the morning and raining.

Even on non-rainy weekend mornings, streets in Scandinavian suburbs are desolate. After several minutes' walk – in the wrong direction, as I found out later – I spotted a shop that was open. The shop sold fresh salmon and shrimp. Fortunately for me, the Albanian assistant to the Danish shop-owner spoke some English. After contacting someone by his cell phone, he was able to give me the right direction to the embassy. I thanked him profusely for his help.

The pink color of the embassy building reminded me of the beautiful Pink City of Rajasthan. There begins and ends anything good I can say about it, though. There was not a single soul around the embassy. And there was not a single piece of decoration that would suggest that the place was about to celebrate the most important event in the history of the country it represents.

I hung around for a while, reading notices on the door, one of which referred to the previous day. It said that the place would be closed on August 14, "on the occasion of Janmashtami," Lord Krishna's birthday. "But what about India's birthday?" That was the immediate question that I had.

A few minutes later, I saw a man wearing a turtle-neck jacket, which made it clear that he worked for the Indian government, and with a bunch of keys in his hand, approach the door. He looked 50-something but had yet to learn how to smile. He did return my "Good Morning," though, but in a tone that suggested that I was being a nuisance.

"Is there going to be any celebration here today?" I asked him.

"Yes," he said. "It begins at ten o'clock."

I was disappointed. I had to be at the airport well before 10. I headed for the train station, to go back to the hotel and pick up my bags.

August 15 Is a Holiday in Parts of Germany

The experience I had this morning was in striking contrast to the one I had a year ago today. On August 15, 2008, I was in Munich, Germany.

The day was set aside for a visit to the Dachau Concentration Camp Memorial. Like today, last year also, India was very much on my mind when I woke up in the morning and during most of the day.

Dachau is 10 miles away from Munich. I was at the main train station, waiting for the train – S2 – that would take me there. When no S2 train showed up for nearly 30 minutes, I asked a lady standing nearby what the problem could be.

"Oh, you didn't hear the announcement?" she said. "It's also shown here," she added, pointing to the electronic display board in front of us. "Today, S2 trains are leaving from another platform because of track work."

Both the display and the announcement were in German. I confessed to my ignorance and then added, "Before I come to Germany next time, I will make sure that I acquire at least a smattering of the language."

"Don't' be apologetic," she said, "many of my friends don't speak any language other than German. Today is a holiday. Most of the repair work on rail-tracks is done on holidays and weekends. Your train will be leaving from that area." She pointed to an area outside the main section of the station. It was a few minutes' walk from where we were standing.

"August 15 is a holiday in Germany, too!" I exclaimed to the lady. "I am thrilled to hear that."

"No, only in this part of Germany." Looking at the train that was approaching, she added, "Nice talking to you." She walked toward the train.

As her train started moving, she once again indicated, this time with her thumb, the area from which Dachau-bound trains would be departing.

There were no escalators in that area. One had to walk up a few steps to reach the platform level. When I saw a woman struggling to walk up, carrying a stroller with her baby still seated in it, I rushed toward her and caught one end of the stroller. "Let me help you," I told her.

"That's so kind of you," she said.

When we reached the platform, I told her where I was going and asked whether I was on the right platform.

"I am taking the same train," she said. "I will be getting off before you." Then she added, with a lovely smile, "Yes, you are on the right platform."

Once inside the train and comfortably seated side by side, I told her, "I never knew that parts of Germany care for India this much."

"What do you mean?" she said.

"Aren't you enjoying your holiday today?" I asked her.

"Yes, I am," she replied. "That's why I am visiting my mother today. She is a practicing Catholic. Though I am not religious, I make her happy by visiting her on holidays like this one. I like India. So do most of my friends. But this holiday has nothing to do with India."

"How stupid of me," I said. "Today is India's Independence Day. I thought the holiday is in observance of that."

"No," she said, "it is in observance of the Assumption of the Virgin Mary. Catholics believe that the Virgin Mary went to Heaven on August 15."

She also told me that it was a holiday only in the two Catholic-majority provinces of Germany – Bavaria and Saarland. Munich is the capital of Bavaria. The Catholic-majority provinces enjoy three more paid holidays than the rest of the country. The other two are January 6 (Epiphany) and November 1 (All Saints Day).

After thanking the young lady for the new piece of information, I added, "See, I am an agnostic."

"I am an agnostic, too," she replied. "But that doesn't stop me from enjoying holidays like this, especially when they are paid holidays."

I laughed, appreciating her candor. "Some of my best friends are Catholics," I told her. "They seldom miss an opportunity to chastise me on my agnosticism and to give me sermons on Christianity and the Bible. But not once did any of them mention this Virgin Mary connection to the day of India's Independence. I had to travel half the world to learn about it, that too from an agnostic German."

"Life is a continuous process of learning," she said. "Isn't it wonderful?"

"And that's why I love traveling," I told her.

As the train approached the next station, she got up, saying, "I have to get off here."

"Let me help you with the stroller," I said, "you carry the baby." As we walked toward the door, I added, "Whenever you have to climb steps next time, make sure that you un-strap the baby from the stroller and carry him separately."

"I like that chastising tone," she said, adding, "You remind me of my ex-husband."

She said the last part with a squint and an endearing smile. I didn't have time to explore what that squint meant. We waved good-bye to each other when the train started moving. I went back to my seat, feeling great.

●

That happened a year ago today. Throughout the past year, the new piece of information about August 15 that I received from the young German has been the subject of a quiz I tried on my Catholic-Indian friends. I might have done it a dozen times by now. The quiz would begin thus:

"What do India and Virgin Mary have in common?"

When my friends looked puzzled, I would scold them, with the superior air of a priest: "What kind of Catholics are you? You give me lectures on the Bible at the drop of a hat. And this simple Biblical fact you have to learn from an infidel! Shame on you."

"OK, we admit we don't know," my friends would say, "What is the connection between the two? Tell us."

"You know the date of India's Independence," I would begin my answer.

"Oh, we get it," my friends would stop me from continuing. Then they would add, "Now, tell us: Whom did you get this information from?"

With great relish, I would tell them what happened to me in Munich, on August 15, 2008. I always made it a point not to omit from my narration the squint and the smile with which the lady referred to her ex-husband.

•

CORRECTION: John Moran, a friend of mine who lives in New York, has this to say about my quiz: "I am a non-theist Catholic and want to 'correct' one thing: the Assumption is nowhere in the Bible; it is part of 'Tradition,' which for Catholics is equal to the Bible as a source of divine revelation. How knotty these fine points about religion can be!" Thank you, John. Thank you for correcting me.

25

One of South Africa's Ruling Class Then, a Migrant Farm Worker in Texas Now

I landed in Johannesburg on a cool December morning in 2010. Though December is summertime in South Africa, it was unusually cool on the morning I landed there. My connection flight to Cape Town was at 12 noon, which meant that I had nearly four hours to kill, at the Johannesburg airport.

Cape Town was going to be the starting point of a seven-day tour of South Africa, organized by a travel company in New York. All 36 members of the tour group, all of them from the U.S., were going to meet at the Cape Town airport, to be escorted by a representative of the tour company.

After a 15-hour, nonstop flight from New York to Johannesburg, most of which I slept through, I badly needed a coffee. I headed to a nearby coffee shop as soon as I completed immigration and customs formalities.

I was slightly disappointed to learn that the coffee would cost two U.S. dollars. That was as much as it cost me at New York's JFK airport. In terms of per capita GDP, South Africa is 76th in the world. An item of daily consumption by an average South African costing as much as it does in the U.S., whose per capita GDP is sixth in the world, did come as a surprise to me. I decided to have it anyway.

There was another problem, though: The lowest-denomination dollar bill I had with me was that of 20. "Can I get the balance in U.S. dollars?" I asked the young lady at the cash register.

"No," she said.

"In that case, can I get the same exchange rate as at any bank?"

"No, we change it at 5.95 rand per dollar."

"That's way below the official rate," I told her. The official rate at the time was 6.83 South African rand per U.S. dollar.

She wanted to be helpful, however, and suggested that I go to a nearby bank and change the dollar. "You will get a better rate there," she said.

But all the banks were inside the restricted area I had just come out of. A white South African was standing nearby watching what was going on.

"Let me pay for your coffee," he said. "Just to pay for one coffee you don't have to go back and go through all that trouble now. You can exchange your dollars in the city, later."

"Could you take this twenty-dollar bill and give me some rand?" I asked him. "I don't mind losing money to another human being, especially one who is so generous to a total stranger."

"You can change the money later," he said. "This coffee is on me. I insist."

"Thank you. Could I sit with you and chat? My flight, to Cape Town, is only at noon."

"My flight is at eleven-thirty. Let's go and sit there," he said, pointing to an empty table away from the sales counter.

"You might have thought that I was being petty," I said, sitting at the table across from him. "It is not a question of how much the coffee costs or what the official dollar-to-rand exchange rate is. It has been my experience all over the world that when it comes to dealing with tourists, the price of everything goes up. I learned the hard way the need to be extra cautious."

"I offered to pay for the coffee," he said, "because I didn't want you to go back inside, looking for a bank or an ATM machine. You will have to go through the security formalities all over again. You and I know what a hassle it is."

"It's very kind of you," I said.

We introduced ourselves to each other and started talking. He was from a small rural community in South Africa, an hour's flight from Johannesburg plus two hours' drive from the airport. He did mention the name of his village and of the small town in which the airport is. I don't remember them because I never heard of them before. He said he had just arrived from Washington, D.C.

From the way he spoke English, I could tell that he was not of British descent. I guessed that he was an Afrikaner, a white South African of Dutch descent. The Dutch were the first Europeans to colonize South Africa. The colonization began in the early 17th century. The English and the French followed later.

The tiny, white Afrikaner minority ruled South Africa from 1948 to 1994. The political and social system which prevailed in the country during that period, and which enabled this 10-percent white minority to rule over the 90-percent non-white majority, was called – yes, you guessed it right – apartheid.

Apartheid Means 'Apartness'

Apartheid in Afrikaans, one of the official languages of South Africa, means separateness or 'apartness.' Derived from the Dutch language, Afrikaans is the mother tongue of Afrikaners, who were the architects of apartheid. During the apartheid rule, all non-whites, especially the native blacks who constitute 80 percent of the population, were separated from positions of power and privileges, and permanently relegated to an inferior status.

"What language do you speak at home?" I asked.

"Afrikaans," he said.

"I guessed so," I told him. "Did you go to the U.S. on a vacation?"

"No," he said, "I am a seasonal farm worker in Texas."

The answer came to me as a surprise. There are about 3.5 million seasonal farm workers in the U.S. Most of them are Latinos – from

Mexico and nearby South American countries. I had never expected an Afrikaner, who had been part of the ruling class in South Africa until a few years earlier, to go all the way to the U.S. to take up job as a migrant farm worker.

Unlike most Latino workers who sneak into the U.S. during the farming season, however, he went there with proper documents. He showed me the temporary-worker visa stamped on his passport. He said that both the work on the Texas farm and the visa were arranged by a Johannesburg employment agency. He was on his way home, after finishing his four-month stint.

"This has been the pattern of my life in the past four years," he said. "Work in Texas for four months. Come home and spend two months with my wife. Then back to Texas, again."

His wife was a schoolteacher. "We have no children," he added. "Because I am a temporary worker, I didn't want my wife to quit her job and join me in Texas. Moreover, there will be nothing left after feeding two mouths in the U.S. So we decided to put up with this arrangement for some time." Back in his village, he had already bought a small piece of land. But "it will take years for the land to produce anything," he said.

Another reason why he decided to leave his wife behind was that his work on the Texas farm was not conducive to any family life. He worked 16 hours a day, seven days a week.

"You have been working sixteen hours a day, every day, for four months!" I exclaimed.

"Yes," he said, casually, giving me the impression that it was no big deal.

"You might have made a fortune in overtime."

"No, I get nine dollars an hour. No overtime."

"What?" I said, in shock, "I know nine dollars is more than the legal minimum wage in the U.S. But do you know that under the U.S. law, you are entitled to overtime for every hour you put in above forty hours every week?"

"I heard something about overtime, but don't know how much. I don't know whether my employment agency in Johannesburg is collecting it. In any case, I wouldn't fight for it. What I have now is a blessing, compared with what I was going through before I got it."

Before he became a migrant worker in Texas, he was jobless. Before he became jobless, he was the owner of a convenience store. "After the country came under black-majority rule, many black-owned stores came up in my village," he said. "I started losing customers and money. When I could not take the loss anymore, I decided to close my business. See, I am part of the three-percent white minority in my village."

I could discern some sadness in his tone when he uttered the last sentence. He continued: "After I closed my business, we survived on my wife's income. In a way it's good that we don't have children. Otherwise, they would have suffered. You know people like me have no future in South African villages." Once again, there was a tinge of sadness in his tone. "So when I saw an advertisement about this job, in a Johannesburg newspaper, I applied for it and got it. Maybe I got it because, years ago, as a teenager, I had worked on my father's small farm. I did mention that experience in my application. My father declared bankruptcy even before I completed high school. Too much drinking. I couldn't afford to go to college. So I opened a small store. That's a long story."

Soon after he arrived in Texas, he realized that the experience he had on his father's farm, which produced fruits and vegetables, was not of much use on his new job. On the 16,000-acre Texas farm, which grows cotton and corn, everything is done on a mega-scale, with machines. So his new boss decided to use him as a truck driver. The owner didn't live on the farm. He lived in Dallas. A supervisor, who lived on the farm with his wife and two children, ran the operation. "He shouts at us a lot," he said. "But he is a good man."

The farm is near the southern border of Texas. "There were times when I fell asleep on the truck, almost hitting the fence that separates our farm from the neighboring one. Other times, I could let the truck run for miles and miles unattended, when I would be reading newspapers, preparing coffee, or eating my lunch."

The only time he and his fellow workers got a break during their four-month, 16-hour-a-day, work was when it rained. Sometimes it rained for days and days, he said, when they would stay at home. That was the only time when they got a chance to use the living room, watch TV and chat with housemates. Twelve workers shared a house, which the farm-owner provided rent-free.

"We were not all that happy about the break we got," he said, with a smile. "When we didn't work, we didn't get paid." Sometimes, for several days in a row, he and his fellow farm workers had to go without pay.

He said he decided to continue this grueling work pattern for four more years. It was his hope that if he endured it for another four years, he would be able to save enough money to buy a house. He was hoping to buy it in a nearby town and move there, after disposing of whatever he had in his village. "People like me have no future in the villages of South Africa," he said, repeating the point he made earlier.

Our conversation was interrupted by an announcement on the PA system, asking passengers on his flight to proceed to the aircraft. I was disappointed that the conversation ended when it started to become interesting.

I wanted to give him something as a parting gift. I couldn't think of anything of value in my bag. I opened it and riffled through the contents anyway. Yes, there were two packets of biscuits among them. I took them out, opened one packet and shared it with him. To reassure him that it was safe to eat it, I started eating first.

"It's good," he said, tasting a biscuit himself.

I gave him the unopened packet and said, "Please share it with your wife when you reach home. I picked it up at an Indian store in my New York neighborhood." Pointing to the word "Parle" on the packet, I added, "It's a famous company in India. This brand is very popular among Indians."

"It's very kind of you," he said, looking at the packet. He held it as though it were something precious. There was a glow on his face when he said, "Yes, I will share it with my wife. I am sure she will like it."

We exchanged our email addresses and promised to stay in touch. I gave him a warm hug and said, "This conversation has been a real treat."

●

Many things went through my mind, as I watched him walk toward the departure gate. I once again thought about the glow his face exuded when he held the packet of biscuit. Its material value was only a few cents. But the role it played in building a rapport between two total strangers, belonging to two totally different cultures, was invaluable.

I thought about apartheid, too. He being an Afrikaner, it was but natural for anyone to think about it. But I found it difficult to associate a fine human being like him with that much-detested system. The words he uttered sadly – "People like me have no future in the villages of South Africa" – reverberated in my mind. I asked myself: "Did the architects of apartheid ever imagine when they brought their country under that abominable system that, one day, some of their own would become its unintended victims? That some of those who once owned the land would one day be forced to leave it, looking for jobs as migrant farm workers in a foreign land?"

26

Greece May Be in a Financial Mess, But Greeks Are Resilient and Decent

"Eight-Day Classic Greece." That's how the Pennsylvania-based company characterized the tour. And classic Greece was the main motivation for my joining the 30-member group from the U.S. that went on the tour.

One of these days, I will be writing about the monuments and sites that represent classic Greece, which I visited during the eight-day tour that started on June 12, 2013. This piece, however, is about the Greece of today (2013), and about the very ordinary Greeks who made my tour a memorable experience.

The Greece of today is in a financial mess. But the Greeks are a resilient people. In spite of the economic woes brought upon them by the stupid policies followed by their leaders, they have remained basically decent and honest. After all, they are the descendants of those who gave the world the gifts of democracy and the Olympics. They know the importance of being fair and of playing by the rule in the conduct of their day-to-day life.

A clue to what we could be witnessing in the following days came from our tour guide on the day we landed in Athens, the Greek capital. The guide ended her orientation talk with a warning that it was not a good day to go around the city on our own. According to the tour schedule, after the orientation talk, we were free to do whatever we liked the rest of the day. But anything untoward could happen that day, the guide said, because various labor unions were planning some protest demonstrations in the city.

The warning made many in the tour group stay put in the hotel. I told a lady who was sitting next to me during the orientation talk that protest demonstrations wouldn't intimidate a person born and brought up in the southern Indian state of Kerala. "I grew up watching them almost every day," I told her, a nurse practitioner from Philadelphia. "I even participated in some of them. I can't wait to see what is going on outside. Would you like to join me?" She happily grabbed the offer.

We walked toward Syntagma Square, about five minutes' walk from the hotel where we were staying. The square, in front of the Parliament building, is one of the places in Athens where protest rallies are usually held. Lately, such rallies have been held frequently in most Greek cities. People have been taking to the streets every time their government imposed a new set of austerity measures on them. The austerity measures are linked to the financial mess mentioned above. How did both come about?

For several years, the Greek government had been irresponsible in spending and not serious about generating revenue. Tax evasion had almost become a norm. Government employees were given huge holiday bonuses, making them in effect recipients of 14 months' salary for 12 months' work. Powerful labor unions have made it almost impossible to get rid of superfluous and incompetent employees. Many of them got their jobs through political favors, jobs-for-votes schemes or pure nepotism. As of 2009, Greece's civil service had 970,000 employees, accounting for a third of the country's work force. In a country of 11 million, that is a jarringly disproportionate number.

On the Brink of Bankruptcy

All this brought Greece to the brink of bankruptcy by early 2010. The national debt of 300 billion euros (394 billion U.S. dollars) was about to exceed the gross domestic product by 20 percent.

Greece being part of the European Union, and also of the euro zone, its economic collapse would be disastrous to both, and also to the world economy. In fact, in late April 2010, when such a collapse was seen as a possibility, its impact was felt half the world away: on Wall Street, New York, Dow Jones Industrial Average dropped 338 points, causing a loss of about $3,000 in the investment portfolio of an average U.S. investor.

The Greek government was forced to seek outside help. The European Central Bank, the European Commission, and the International Monetary Fund came to its rescue. They came up with a bailout package worth 110 billion euros ($146 billion). The loan was to be given in three installments, over a three-year period.

Of course, the aid package came with strict conditions attached to it. To receive each installment, the Greek government had to convince the troika of lenders that it had put in place the set of austerity measures stipulated by them. The measures involved cutting the country's budget deficit to 3 percent of the GDP by 2014; cutting salaries of public-sector workers, including lawmakers; eliminating 150,000 civil service positions; increasing taxes; drastically reducing public spending; and so on.

According to many economists, especially those belonging to the Keynesian school, adopting stringent austerity measures when the economy is in recession is a short-sighted policy. But the Greek government had to do it to qualify for the loan, which alone would keep the country's economy afloat. As the then-finance minister George Papaconstantinou said soon after signing the bailout agreement, on May 1, 2010, the choice was between "destruction" of the country and saving it.

No sooner had the government announced the first set of austerity measures than the public rose in revolt against them. The May Day celebrations of 2010 were marred by clashes between demonstrators and police and by destruction of public property.

Unlike in previous protests, in which people's ire was directed also at the country's bloated bureaucracy, the protests we were warned about on the day of our arrival was, in a way, in solidarity with a section of government employees. Effective 11 p.m. the day before, Prime Minister Antonis Samaras had ordered the closing of the Hellenic Broadcasting Corporation. By closing the state-owned television and radio broadcasting outfit, known as ERT, he was hoping to eliminate 2,900 government jobs.

Latest Austerity Measures

Getting rid of broadcast employees was part of the latest austerity plan attached to the next loan installment, which is $11.4 billion. To convince the lenders that it was serious about the austerity plan, the Greek Parliament had passed a law, in April this year, to eliminate 15,000 civil service jobs by the end of 2014. The shutting down of ERT was done in pursuance of that law.

As soon as the shutdown was ordered, 3,000 people, including ERT employees, gathered outside the broadcaster's headquarters and vowed to stage a sit-in until the government rescinded the order.[****]

The nurse practitioner from Philadelphia, with whom I was wandering around, and I were happy to hear that the day's protests would be confined to the premises of ERT, far away from where we were. We decided to limit our wandering to areas adjacent to Syntagma Square. A teeny-weeny jewelry store caught my friend's attention. She told me that she was an impulsive shopper. We ambled into the store. While my friend checked out various items, we engaged the store owner, a young man in his early twenties, in an interesting conversation.

The store was family-owned, he said. It was started, before he was born, by his grandfather. All the items in the store were handmade, by members of his family. He would soon be inheriting the family business, he said. He was sorry for his friends who finished the four-year college with him this summer. "They don't have a job," he added, "and the prospect of finding one is bleak. The unemployment rate

---

[****] *To get slightly ahead of our story, in less than a month, ERT was back on the air. Apart from ERT employees' sit-in, it took intervention by the country's highest court for the government to rescind its earlier decision.*

among those who are fresh out of colleges and schools is 60 percent. In the country as a whole, the unemployment rate is 27 percent."

By then, my friend had decided to buy a pair of earrings. She asked the price and also the tax. The tax was 23 percent. When the man handed her the receipt, she pointed out that he had forgotten to add the tax.

"Oh, that's included in the price," he said. "We call it value-added tax."

We were impressed by the man's honesty and talked about it as we came out of the store. We both are frequent travelers. Ripping off tourists is a norm in most countries, even countries that are not going through the kind of hardship that Greece was. We both have been victims of such rip-offs. Naturally, we were touched by the decency and honesty displayed by the young man.

I noticed that honesty and decency in many more Greeks during my interactions with them in the following days of the tour. I also noted that, no matter what the hardship, they have not lost their sense of community and are committed to helping one another. That quality was more noticeable in Greek villages, which were hit harder than cities by the government-imposed, Troika-mandated austerity plan. One day, the entire tour group had the good fortune to benefit from that noble quality of Greek villagers.

Lunch at a Farmer's House

In many villages, public schools have become the casualties of the austerity plan that calls for drastic cuts in government spending. Some schools are kept open through contributions made by local communities. One day, when it came time for lunch, our tour guide made a surprise announcement. She told us that the day's lunch would be a gift to us from the tour company, Gate 1 Travel. It was the company's way of supporting a village community that had fallen on hard times, she said. The offer sounded sweeter when she said that the lunch would be prepared by a local farmer's family and that we would be having it at the farmer's house. The lunch money the company paid would go to the community as a whole. The company picked this particular village because, in a fire in 2007, it lost 36 of its houses; and this particular farmer, because, in the same fire, he lost several head of his sheep.

The name of the village is Kuchohera, which our guide told us meant the injured hand. The host family's contribution came in the form of the manual labor of the man of the house, his wife and his two children. The wife proved to be an excellent cook and her husband an excellent cheese-maker. The cheese we had was made out of the milk from his own sheep. Their two sons didn't speak a word of English. But the meticulous way in which they took care of our little-little needs touched our hearts more than a thousand words would.

I have taken a lot of tours conducted by Gate 1. A few of them did disappoint me. But the hospitality and lunch I enjoyed at the home of a farmer in Kuchohera village in Greece has more than made up for all the disappointments I had in the past. Thank you, Gate 1.

The Greek government and the troika of international lenders, especially the IMF which is the chief architect of the austerity plan that is partly responsible for the hardships ordinary Greeks are experiencing now, can learn a lesson or two from the resilience, ingenuity and compassion of village communities in Greece.

PICTURES

1

A Typical Weekend Scene at San Telmo, Buenos Aires

The tango dance originated in Argentina. The picture shows a typical Sunday evening scene at street corners of the San Telmo neighborhood of Buenos Aires, the Argentine capital. The performers sometimes pick partners from among spectators and give them a crash course in tango before forcing them to dance.

2

Avenida 9 de Julio, Buenos Aires

Avenida 9 de Julio (July 9 Avenue), Buenos Aires. It is the widest
avenue the author has seen in any city anywhere in the world. The
obelisk in the middle is a city landmark. It was built in 1936 to
commemorate the 400th anniversary of the founding of Buenos
Aires. *(The picture is reproduced by courtesy of images.google.com.)*

3

Ipanema and Copacabana – Two Beautiful Beaches of Rio de Janeiro

Ipanema (above) and Copacabana (seen beyond the bay-like body of water, in front of rows of luxury hotels and residential buildings). The two beaches are separated by a small piece of elevated land jutting out into the sea.

4

On a Pleasure Cruise, Off
the Brazilian Coast

The odd man in the picture is the author. He is enjoying a boat ride, off the
coast of Rio de Janeiro, courtesy his Brazilian host. Others in the picture
are the host's wife and family friends. All of them, except the author, are
getting ready for a swim in the blue waters of the Atlantic. Because the
author doesn't know how to swim, he has an excuse to keep his T-shirt on.

5

Hunchback and Sugar Loaf

The picture captures the beauty of two major tourist destinations in Rio de Janeiro – Pão d'Açúcar (left) and Corcovado. The statue is that of Jesus Christ. Built on the uppermost spot of the Corcovado Mountain, it is so huge that one can see it from miles and miles afar. Corcovado in Portuguese means hunchback. Viewed from the city, the mountain does look like a hunchback.

The dome-shaped rock, to the left, is the Sugar Loaf Mountain (Pão d'Açúcar, in Portuguese). (*The picture is reproduced by courtesy of* Wikimedia.)

6

In Front of Imperial Palace, Beijing

The author (far left) with the rest of the nine-member tour group from the U.S., in front of the Imperial Palace in Tiananmen Square, Beijing. The picture of Mao Zedong, at the entrance, is so large that it can be seen from the other end of Tiananmen Square. The square is as large as 60 soccer fields put together.

7

The Temple of Heaven, Beijing

The Temple of Heaven was founded in Beijing in 1420, during the reign of Emperor Yongle of the Ming Dynasty, for Chinese emperors to worship Heaven. The principal buildings in the 273-hectare complex include the Altar of Prayer for Good Harvests, Imperial Vault of Heaven and Circular Mound Altar. Until 1911, 22 emperors of the Ming and Qing Dynasties had worshiped Heaven and conducted ceremonial sacrifices at this temple. In 1911, the Republic of China banned all ceremonial sacrifices and it ceased to be a place of worship and sacrifices. In 1918, the sprawling complex, including the well-maintained parks in it, was reopened, this time as a window to a part of China's past and a place of tourist attraction. Now, tourists to Beijing mark it as one of the must-see places. *(The picture is reproduced by courtesy of* chinadiscoverytours.com.*)*

8

The Great Wall of China

The author, on his way to the Great Wall of China. Though the wall has
a history of more than 2,000 years, most of it was built during the rule of
the Ming Dynasty (1368-1644). The original purpose of building it was
to protect the empire from foreign invaders. Now it is one of the greatest
tourist attractions in China. In 1987, the UNESCO added the Great Wall
to its list of World Heritage Sites. Stretching from the Hushan Mountain
in the east to Jiayuguan Pass in the west, the wall passes through deserts,
grasslands, mountains, and plateaus. Over the years, many sections of
the wall have deteriorated and disappeared. The Badaling section of the
wall, 43 miles northwest of Beijing, was rebuilt in the late 1950s. One
of the greatest thrills the author had during his tour of Beijing was that,
thanks to the rebuilding of the Badaling section, he was able to walk
at least half a mile on the 13,170-mile-long Great Wall of China.

9

China Celebrates May Day
With a Fashion Parade

A fashion parade in Shanghai, China, on May 1, 2002. Many tourists were surprised that a fashion parade, which Mao Zedong would associate with "decadent capitalism," should be part of May Day celebrations in China, the only communist country of any cloud left in the world, and one founded by Mao himself.

10

Pudong, Shanghai, as Seen at Night

Pudong, Shanghai, as seen by the author while on a night cruise
along the Huangpu River. Built in the 1990s, Pudong is the special
economic zone of Shanghai. The building, with a spire on top (for radio
and TV antennas), is the 1,535-foot-tall Oriental Pearl Tower. It was
the tallest structure in all of China until 2007, when the 1,614-foot-
tall Shanghai World Financial Centre surpassed it in height.

11

Nanjing Road, World's Busiest Shopping Street

Nanjing Road, Shanghai, China. With over a million visitors a day, this for-pedestrians-only street is said to be the busiest shopping area in the world. (*The picture is reproduced by courtesy of* chinapage.com.)

12

A Morning Ritual in Luang Prabang, Laos

Buddhist monks from monasteries in Luang Prabang, Laos, going through the morning ritual of receiving offerings from devotees.

13

Traffic Jam in Bangalore City, at Night

The two illuminated buildings in the picture, at the busy intersection of St. John's Church Road and Haines Road, in the Coles Park area of Bangalore, rent out spaces for special events, mostly weddings. This is a typical scene at night when such an event takes place in the building to the left. Guests at the event convert the public road into a private parking lot, leaving hardly any room for city buses and private motorists to pass through. When a frustrated neighborhood resident complained about this egregious violation to the traffic police on beat at the intersection, he was given a phone number to call and report the matter and dismissed as a nuisance.

14

Bangalore, Where Traffic Encroaches on Sidewalks

This is what the same St. John's Church Road-Haines Road intersection, mentioned in the previous page, looks like on a typical working day. As one can see, the road and sidewalk are at the same level, making it easy for motorists to encroach on the sidewalk, leaving no room for pedestrians. A row of cars is seen permanently parked on the sidewalk. The cars belong to some of the neighborhood residents and to the owner of the building to the left which rents out space for weddings and other celebrations. Other neighborhood residents are appalled that this blatant violation takes place under the very noses of the traffic police who are on duty at the intersection most of the time. The picture above and this caption are true of any busy intersection in Bangalore.

15

Where Road Doubles as Dump, in Bangalore

An eyesore outside Coles Park, in the Fraser Town area of Bangalore: garbage dumped on the road and sidewalk. Stray cows and stray dogs are often seen helping themselves to whatever is edible to them. Poor people rummage it to salvage whatever is of any value to them. Concerned Bangaloreans ask: "Is it too much to expect the city to keep dumpsters in places like this?" The stench emanating from the garbage notwithstanding, the health-conscious in the neighborhood use Coles Park, one of the many beautiful parks in the city, for morning and evening walks and jogs.

16

The Sultan Ahmet Mosque, Istanbul, Turkey

The Sultan Ahmet Mosque, named after the Ottoman emperor who built it (between 1609 and 1616), in Istanbul, Turkey. It is better known as the Blue Mosque, for the blue tiles that adorn its interior walls. The mosque is one of the main tourist attractions in Istanbul.

17

Monument that Commemorates Mexico's War of Independence

El Angel, a monument in Mexico City, built at the turn of the
20th century to commemorate Mexico's war of independence from
Spain. One interpretation of the Angel's looking northward is that
Mexicans are more wary of Americans, their northern neighbors,
than of Spaniards, who conquered them in the 16th century.

18

Statue of Diana the Huntress, in Mexico City

Statue of Diana the Huntress, in Mexico City. Many Mexicans say that the arrow is made to point to the north intentionally. It is aimed at the United States, they say. *(The picture is reproduced by courtesy of* Wikimedia.*)*

19

A Memorial Bridge on Austro-Hungarian Border

The Bridge at Andau. The original bridge, which Hungarians had used to escape to Austria when Soviet tanks rolled into their country to crush their revolution, was destroyed by the Soviets. This one was built in its place later, mainly as a memorial to the revolution – the Hungarian Revolution of 1956.

20

Monument to Hungarian Revolution

This lookout-like structure is another memorial to the Hungarian Revolution of 1956. It was built by students of the University of Sopron to thank Austrians for the "touching help and hospitality" they provided to the escapees from Soviet tyranny.

21

Manneken Pis, a Tourist Attraction in Brussels

Manneken Pis, a statue showing a little child urinating, is a big tourist attraction in Brussels, the capital of Belgium. The statue stirred some controversy in Bombay, in the late 1960s, when Air India used it in an advertising campaign to promote its newly-introduced flights to Brussels.

22

Karl Johans Gate in Oslo, Norway

Karl Johans Gate, a for-pedestrians-only street in Oslo, Norway, as it looked on an early morning. The street and sidewalks get crowded in the evening with strollers and alfresco diners. The building at the far end is the Royal Palace of Norway.

23

A Tourist Boat Heading to a Nearby Fjord, in Oslo, Norway

Cruising through one of the fjords is a pleasure most visitors to Norway make it a point to give themselves. The picture above shows a tourist boat heading to a nearby fjord, in Oslo, the capital of Norway.

24

Myrdal Train Station, at Midway Between Oslo and Bergen

The Myrdal train station, which is about half-way from Oslo to Bergen, in Norway. Tourists to Norway, who plan to go on the famous Aurlandsfjord cruise, get off at this station and take a train bound for Flam. The mountain range in the background gives the Myrdal station an exotic look.

25

A Panoramic View of Bergen, Norway

Bergen, Norway's most beautiful and second-largest city, as seen from the top of one of the seven mountains surrounding it. A funicular ride takes one to the top of the mountain. If "Norway's greatest claim to scenic fame is its deep and lush fjords," as the well-known travel writer Rick Steves puts it, Bergen is the "gateway to the fjords." As is the case with Bergen on most days, it was raining on the day the author visited it. Bergen is nicknamed "the City of Rain." But the rain neither dampens the spirits of its visitors nor tarnishes its beauty. A joke in Bergen about its perennial rain goes thus: "A tourist asks a local boy if it ever stops raining. 'I don't know,' replies the boy, 'I am only twelve.'"

26

Picture of Dead Prisoners at Dachau Concentration Camp Memorial

This picture is displayed in the photo section of the Dachau Concentration Camp Memorial, near Munich, Germany. The caption to the picture reads: "Dead prisoners outside the death chamber near the Infirmary Block B, after the liberation [of the camp by American soldiers, on April 29, 1945]."

27

Dark Cells of Dachau Concentration Camp

This is one of the several rows of dark cells in the Dachau Concentration Camp. On the wall of Cell No. 19 hangs a note written by its occupant, Erwin Gostner. The English translation of the note reads: "Four months in the Bunker, four months' detention in darkness, four months with hot food only every fourth day! Time crawls by. I only count every fourth day, and I'm amazed when the food comes and wakes me up – I'm in a state of trance."

28

The Mermaid, a Big Tourist Attraction in Copenhagen

The author, in front of the Mermaid statue in Copenhagen, Denmark.
The Mermaid is a big tourist attraction in the Danish capital.

29

Man-to-Seal, Mouth-to-Mouth Fish Feeding

Two South Africans found an ingenious way of making a living: Entertaining tourists by demonstrating the art of man-to-seal, mouth-to-mouth fish feeding.

30

Syntagma Square, Athens, Greece

Syntagma Square, in front of the Parliament building in Athens, Greece.
Protest rallies in the Greek capital are usually held in this square.

www.ingramcontent.com/pod-product-compliance
Lightning Source LLC
Chambersburg PA
CBHW041626140626
46547CB00030B/1067